A NEW STYLE
ITALIAN GRAMMAR

GUIDA ALLE STRUTTURE DELLA LINGUA ITALIANA
&
VOCABULARY LISTS BY TOPIC

LEONARDO ORIOLO

**EUROPEAN
SCHOOLBOOKS
PUBLISHING**

Alla memoria di mio padre

ISBN 0 85048 300 X

European Schoolbooks Publishing Ltd
The Runnings
Cheltenham
GL51 9PQ
England

INTRODUCTORY NOTE

This book is best used in conjunction with the companion volume "Pronti ... Via! The Italian Handbook" which provides essential practice material in easily accessible form. The New Style Italian Grammar can however also stand in its own right as a concise reference guide to the fundamental structures of the Italian language.

It is intended primarily for those learning Italian who are already familiar with a number of basic expressions, enabling them to have an elementary conversation in Italian. The learning method assumed here is that the student gains some conversational confidence, and then begins to look in more detail at the grammar.

As far as young learners of school age are concerned, the guide should not be seen as a list of grammatical rules which have to be digested. Instead it should offer support during the phase of enquiry which follows the realisation that some errors seriously interfere with effective communication. The book helps the student to impose some logical order upon the disparate pieces of language which have been absorbed as a result of communicative activities. The layout is clear and makes learning easier.

The basic content has been derived in the main from the practical developments encouraged by the Council of Europe, resulting in the "Threshold Level" or, for Italian, "Livello soglia". It uses the same classification of levels as the syllabuses prepared for the General Certificate of Secondary Education used for pupils aged sixteen and over in the English school system, namely 'basic' and 'higher'. In particular the vocabulary and situations listed in the syllabus of the Northern Examining Association have helped to keep to a minimum the body of notions and functions used as examples, whilst dealing with the maximum number of practical structures.

For students who want to explore beyond the range of notions and functions listed in the Threshold Level and the subsequent school syllabuses this book provides a framework of grammatical analysis. The analysis aims to take account of the way in which living language is put to use as a real communicative tool by speakers and writers of Italian. The systems of rules outlined in the different sections of this guide, and the extensive vocabulary listed by topic and settings, provide the basis for the learner's continuous development of communicative abilities.

I should like to thank all those colleagues who have tried out some of the material, and who have suggested improvements. My gratitude also goes to Maria Galasso, Maria Pia Oliver and John Broadbent for their advice and encouragement. My students also have been extremely helpful and supportive - both those from the European School and from the courses organised by the Italian Consulate. Finally I should like to thank the editor and staff of Links Publications. Emanuela Agni dedicated many hours not only to entering the text into the computer but also to elaborating the layout of the book. Special thanks are due to the editor, Clive Mira-Smith who made the present publication possible and used it to launch the new Pronti Via! series of Italian teaching materials.

Leonardo Oriolo
March 1990

CONTENTS

15. VOCABULARY LISTS BY TOPIC

1. NOUNS (NOMI)

1.1 Gender, Singular and Plural

	SINGULAR	PLURAL	Ending	
MASCULINE	ragazz**o**	ragazz**i**	**-o**	**-i**
FEMININE	ragazz**a**	ragazz**e**	**-a**	**-e**
MASCULINE	getton**e**	getton**i**	**-e**	**-i**
FEMININE	canzon**e**	canzon**i**		

1.2 Common Irregular Nouns (singular-plural)

SINGULAR	PLURAL	
il film	i film	(a) Some nouns don't change in the plural. They are:
lo sport	gli sport	- most words of foreign origin;
il re	i re	
la città	le città	- monosyllables;
l'università	le università	- nouns stressed on the final vowel;
la radio	le radio	
la foto	le foto	- some feminine nouns ending in **-o;**
il brindisi	i brindisi	- nouns ending in **-i.**
il ciclista	i ciclisti	(b) The few masculine nouns ending in **-a**
il clima	i climi	form the plural in **-i.**
il turista	i turisti	
il problema	i problemi	
il telegramma	i telegrammi	
lo **z**io	gli **z**ii	(c) Be careful how you spell the nouns ending in:
lo st**u**dio	gli studi	**-io** (when the **i** is stressed, the plural is **-ii**);
		-io (when the **i** is not stressed, the plural is **-i**);
la spi**a**ggia	le spiagge	**-gia** (when the **i** is not stressed, the plural is **-ge**);
la f**a**ccia	le facce	**-cia** (when the **i** is not stressed, the plural is **-ce**);
la bug**i**a	le bugie	**-gia** (when the **i** is stressed, the plural is **-gie**);
la farmac**i**a	le farmacie	**-cia** (when the **i** is stressed, the plural is **-cie**);
l'amico	gli amici	**-co/-go**
l'asparago	gli asparagi	(their plurals are formed in two different ways:
il cuoco	i cuochi	-ci/gi; -chi/ghi). If in doubt use the dictionary;
l'albergo	gli alberghi	
l'amica	le amiche	**-ca/-ga**
la collega	le colleghe	(their plurals are formed as - **che/ghe**);
il dito	le dita	(d) Remember these irregular nouns.
l'uovo	le uova	
la mano	le mani	

Continued ➡

1.3 **Common Irregular Nouns**
(masculine-feminine)

Masculine		Feminine
lo studente	*student*	la studentessa
il dottore	*doctor*	la dottoressa
il professore	*teacher*	la professoressa
l' attore	*actor*	l' attrice
lo scrittore	*writer*	la scrittrice
il pittore	*artist*	la pittrice
il maschio	*male*	la femmina
l' uomo	*man*	la donna
il celibe	*bachelor*	la nubile
il marito	*husband*	la moglie
il padre	*father*	la madre
il fratello	*brother*	la sorella

1.4 **Common Compound Nouns**
(singular-plural)

Singular		Plural
l' altoparlante	*loudspeaker*	gli altoparlanti
l' arcobaleno	*rainbow*	gli arcobaleni
l' aspirapolvere	*vacuum cleaner*	gli aspirapolvere
la banconota	*banknote*	le banconote
il cacciavite	*screwdriver*	i cacciavite
il capolavoro	*masterpiece*	i capolavori
la cassaforte	*safe*	le casseforti
il cavatappi	*corkscrew*	i cavatappi
il cavolfiore	*cauliflower*	i cavolfiori
la ferrovia	*railway*	le ferrovie
il francobollo	*stamp*	i francobolli
il marciapiede	*pavement*	i marciapiedi
il passaporto	*passport*	i passaporti
il portacenere	*ashtray*	i portacenere
il portafoglio	*wallet*	i portafogli
il salvagente	*lifebelt*	i salvagente
il sottopassaggio	*subway*	i sottopassaggi

Vocabulary:

albergo *hotel*
amico *friend*
brindisi *toast*
bugia *lie*
canzone *song*
ciclista *cyclist*

città *town*
clima *climate*
re *king*
collega *colleague*
cuoco *cook*
dito *finger*

faccia *face*
uovo *egg*
farmacia *pharmacy*
foto *photo*
gettone *token*
mano *hand*

ragazzo *boy*
spiaggia *beach*
studio *study*
università *university*
zio *uncle*

2. ARTICLES (ARTICOLI)

2.1 Definite: (the) il, la, ...

	SINGULAR		PLURAL			
MASC.	**il**	ragazzo	**i**	ragazzi	**il/i**	before a consonant
	lo	studente	**gli**	studenti	**lo/gli**	before s + consonant or z
	l'	albero	**gli**	alberi	**l'/gli**	before a vowel
FEM.	**la**	ragazza	**le**	ragazze	**la/le**	before a consonant
	l'	aula	**le**	aule	**l'/le**	before a vowel

2.2 Indefinite: (a, an) un, una, ...   2.3 Partitive articles: (some, any) del, della, ...

	SINGULAR		PLURAL			
MASC.	**un**	ragazzo	(dei	ragazzi)	**un**	before a consonant or a vowel
	uno	studente	(degli	studenti)	**uno**	before s + consonant or z
FEM.	**una**	ragazza	(delle	ragazze)	**una**	before a consonant
	un'	aula	(delle	aule)	**un'**	before a vowel

e.g.

masculine

il ragazzo	*boy*	i ragazzi	un ragazzo
il libro	*book*	i libri	un libro
il supermercato	*supermarket*	i supermercati	un supermercato
lo studente	*student*	gli studenti	uno studente
lo specchio	*mirror*	gli specchi	uno specchio
lo zio	*uncle*	gli zii	uno zio
l'albero	*tree*	gli alberi	un albero
l'orologio	*watch*	gli orologi	un orologio

feminine:

la ragazza	*girl*	le ragazze	una ragazza
la studentessa	*student*	le studentesse	una studentessa
la zia	*aunt*	le zie	una zia
l'aula	*classroom*	le aule	un'aula
l'isola	*island*	le isole	un'isola

Note

☞ *Lo, **gli** and **uno** are also used in front of the very few words beginning with **x, pn, ps, gn** and the semi-consonant **i**: lo xilofono (xylophone), uno pneumatico (tyre), lo psicologo (psychologist), gli gnocchi ('gnocchi'), lo iogurt (yogurt). In colloquial Italian this rule is followed less strictly, particularly in front of **pn** and **gn**: un pneumatico, i gnocchi.*

☞ ***Gli** may be apostrophised only in front of **i** (although used less and less frequently nowadays): gli indirizzi/gl'indirizzi (addresses), but gli alberghi (hotels), gli occhi (eyes).*

☞ *The partitive article follows the rules of the definite article: del sale, dell'olio, dello zucchero, dei broccoli, degli spinaci, della frutta, dell'insalata, delle banane, (some, any - salt, oil, sugar, broccoli, spinach, fruit, salad, bananas).*

3. ADJECTIVES (AGGETTIVI)

3.1 Regular Formation

	SINGULAR	PLURAL	Ending	
MASCULINE	rosso	rossi	-o	-i
FEMININE	rossa	rosse	-a	-e
MASCULINE AND FEMININE	verde	verdi	-e	-i

e.g. Un ombrello rosso. *A red umbrella*
Una penna rossa. *A red pen*
Un ombrello verde. *A green umbrella*
Una penna verde. *A green pen*

3.2 Agreement

NOUNS		ADJECTIVES
Claudio	è	timido.
Claudio e Mario	sono	timidi.
Carla	è	timida.
Carla e Lucia	sono	timide.
Carla e Mario	sono	timidi.
Carlo e Lucia	sono	timidi.

The adjective agrees in gender and number with the noun it qualifies.

An adjective is given in the masculine plural form if it refers to several nouns of different gender.

3.3 Position of Adjectives

☞ • Adjectives usually follow the noun:
Un libro noioso. Una camera singola. *A boring book. A single room.*
• Sometimes the adjective may be placed either after or before the noun in which case its meaning is often changed according to its position:
È un uomo grande. *He's a big man.* È un grand'uomo. *He's a great man.*

3.4 Common Irregular Adjectives

Bello and **buono** in front of masculine nouns become:

SINGULAR	PLURAL
bel ragazzo	bei ragazzi
bell'albero	begli alberi
bello zaino	begli zaini
buon ragazzo	buoni ragazzi
buon uomo	buoni uomini
buono studente	buoni studenti

Bello follows the rules of the definite article.

In the singular **buono** follows the rules of the indefinite article. The plural is regular.

☞ The feminine of **bello** and **buono** is regular: bella ragazza; belle ragazze; buona ragazza, ...

VOCABULARY
albero *tree*
bello *beautiful, lovely, handsome*
buono *good*

ombrello *umbrella*
penna *pen*
ragazzo *boy*
rosso *red*

timido *shy*
uomo *man*
verde *green*
zaino *rucksack*

3.5 DEMONSTRATIVE ADJECTIVES (AGGETTIVI DIMOSTRATIVI)

3.6 (this) questo, ...

	SINGULAR	PLURAL	
MASCULINE	**questo** libro	**questi** libri	this; these
FEMININE	**questa** penna	**queste** penne	this; these

3.7 (that) quello, ...

	SINGULAR	PLURAL	
MASCULINE	**quel** libro **quello** studente **quell'** albero	**quei** libri **quegli** studenti **quegli** alberi	that; those
FEMININE	**quella** penna **quell'** isola	**quelle** penne **quelle** isole	that; those

Note

Questo	indicates a person or thing	close to the speaker.
Quello		far from the speaker and from the listener.
Codesto		close to the listener.

☞ • *Codesto, codesta, codesti, codeste (that, those) are mainly used in Tuscany or in bureaucratic language.*
   • *The adjective* **questo** *can take an apostrophe in front of a vowel:*
   Quest'inverno (this winter); quest'estate (this summer).
   • *You may sometimes find* **sta** *instead of* **questa***:*
   Stamattina = questa mattina (this morning); stasera = questa sera (this evening).

3. 8 POSSESSIVE ADJECTIVES (AGGETTIVI POSSESSIVI)

	MASCULINE			FEMININE		
	SINGULAR	PLURAL	SINGULAR	PLURAL		
	mio	miei	mia	mie	(my)	
	tuo	tuoi	tua	tue	(your) informal	
	Suo	Suoi	Sua	Sue	(your) formal	
il	suo libro	i suoi libri	la sua penna	le sue penne	(his/her)	
	nostro	nostri	nostra	nostre	(our)	
	vostro	vostri	vostra	vostre	(your)	
	loro	loro	loro	loro	(their)	

3.9 Use of possessive adjectives before terms for family relationships

☞ The articles **il** and **la** are not used in front of possessive adjectives referring to relations:
mio padre *my father*, **sua** madre *his/her mother*, **vostro** fratello *your brother*,
nostra sorella *our sister*, **tuo** marito *your husband*, **mia** moglie *my wife*, ...

☞ The article is used in front of the possessive adjective only if the relations are:
- in the plural: **i miei** fratelli *my brothers*;
- qualified by a suffix: **il mio** fratellino *my little brother*;
- accompanied by another adjective: **il mio** fratello maggiore *my eldest brother*;
- referred to using a term of endearment: **la mia** mamma *my mum*, **il mio** babbo *my dad*.

☞ The article is always used before the possessive adjective **loro**:
il loro figlio *their son*, **i** loro figli *their sons*.

Note

- *The possessive adjective is normally preceded by the definite article.*
- *Possessive adjectives are used less frequently in Italian than in English.*
- *The gender and number of the possessive adjective agree with the accompanying noun and not with the possessor as in English:*
  Questo è il suo libro e questa è la sua penna [di lui]. (This is his book and this is his pen.)
  Questo è il suo libro e questa è la sua penna [di lei]. (This is her book and this is her pen.)

3.10 INDEFINITE ADJECTIVES (AGGETTIVI INDEFINITI)

3.11 (every, some, any) ogni, qualche, qualsiasi

	SINGULAR	
MASCULINE/FEMININE	**ogni**	every, each
	qualche	some, any, a few
	qualsiasi/qualunque	any, every

e.g. **Ogni** volta che vado al mare, incontro Andrea. *Every time I go to the seaside, I meet Andrea.*
Ci vediamo tra **qualche** giorno. *We'll see each other in a few days.*
Qualsiasi/qualunque ristorante va bene. *Any restaurant will do.*

- *Ogni, qualche, qualunque, qualsiasi, are only used as adjectives, never as pronouns.*
- *They are invariable and used only in the singular.*

3.12 (every, no, ...) ciascuno, nessuno

	SINGULAR	
MASCULINE	**ciascuno**	every, each
	nessuno	no, any
FEMININE	**ciascuna**	
	nessuna	

e.g. **Ciascuno** studente deve fare i compiti. *Every student has to do his homework.*
Non ha dato **nessuna** risposta. *He gave no answer.*

- *They take the feminine and are used only in the singular.*
- *They follow the rules of the indefinite article: ciascun libro, ciascun'amica, ciascuno studente, ciascun amico, ciascuna studentessa.*

Continued

3.13 (other, much, ...) altro, molto, ...

	SINGULAR	PLURAL	
MASCULINE	**altro**	**altri**	other, another, more
	molto	**molti**	much, many, a lot
	parecchio	**parecchi**	a good deal of, quite a lot of
	poco	**pochi**	little, few
	tanto	**tanti**	so much, a lot of
	troppo	**troppi**	too much, too many
	tutto	**tutti**	all
FEMININE	**altra**	**altre**	
	molta	**molte**	
	parecchia	**parecchie**	
	poca	**poche**	
	tanta	**tante**	
	troppa	**troppe**	
	tutta	**tutte**	

e.g.   Verrò un **altro** giorno. *I'll come another day.*
Hai **molti** amici italiani? *Do you have many Italian friends?*
È da **parecchio** tempo che non vedo Luca. *I haven't seen Luca for a long time.*
Ci siamo fermati **pochi** giorni. *We stayed there a few days.*
Ha **poca** esperienza. *He has little experience.*
Ho comprato **tanti** libri. *I bought a lot of books.*
Ho preso **troppo** sole. *I caught too much sun.*
Ho rivisto **tutti** gli amici. *I saw all my friends again.*

 They take the feminine and are used both in the singular and plural.

3.14 (some, any, ...) alcuno

Alcuno, alcuna, alcuni, alcune (some, a number of, any, no, ...):

* in the singular follow the rules of the indefinite articles and are used
  only in the negative form: Non ha **alcun'**amica con cui parlare. *She has no friend to talk to.*
* in the plural they mean the same as **qualche**:
  Vorrei comprare **alcuni** libri su Pisa (= qualche libro su Pisa). *I'd like to buy some books on Pisa.*

3.15 INTERROGATIVE ADJECTIVES (AGGETTIVI INTERROGATIVI)

Che?	What? Which?
Quale?	Which?
Quanto?	How much?

3.16 **Che** is invariable and equivalent to **quale, quali**:
Che (=quale) film vuoi vedere? *What film would you like to see?*
Che (=quali) fiori ti piacciono? *Which flowers do you like?*

3.17 **Quale** varies in the plural (**quali**):
Quale materia preferisci? *Which subject do you prefer?*
Quali materie preferisci? *Which subjects do you prefer?*
Quali libri hai letto? *Which books did you read?*

3.18 **Quanto** is variable (quanto, quanta, quanti, quante):
Quanto zucchero vuoi? *How much sugar do you like?*
Quanta frutta hai comprato? *How much fruit did you buy?*
Quanti anni hai? *How old are you?*
Quante materie studi? *How many subjects do you study?*

3.20 Comparative

più ... di	(più ... che)	more ... than
meno ... di	(meno ... che)	less ... than
(tanto) ... quanto (così) ... come		as ... as

e.g.
Ha **più** dischi **di** lei.	*He has more records than she has.*
Carla è **più** giovane **di** lui.	*Carla is younger than he.*
Lui è **meno** giovane **di** Carla.	*He's older than Carla.*
Lei è giovane **quanto** Carla.	*She's as young as Carla.*
Lei è giovane **come** Carla.	*She's as young as Carla.*

☞ **Più/meno ... che** is normally used when the comparison is between:
- two adjectives:
  Quella poltrona è più comoda che pratica. *That armchair is more comfortable than practical.*
- two verbs or two adverbs:
  È **meno** divertente andare a ballare **che** andare al cinema. *Dancing is less enjoyable than going to the cinema.*
  Lui legge **più** velocemente c**h**e correttamente. *He reads more quickly than correctly.*
- in front of a noun or pronoun but only if they are governed by a preposition:
  Perché Daniela è **più** arrogante con me **che** con voi? *Why is Daniela more arrogant with me than with you?*
  Angela ha scritto **più** lettere a Luca c**h**e a Pietro. *Angela has written more letters to Luca than to Pietro.*

☞ In the comparison of equality, **tanto** and **così** are optional and often omitted except when the comparison is between two adjectives:
Nicoletta è **tanto** furba **quanto** intelligente. *Nicoletta is as cunning as she is intelligent.*

Continued

3.21 Superlative

RELATIVE	**il più...**	the most...
	il meno ...	the least...
ABSOLUTE	**-issimo**	very...

e.g. Lui è **il più** simpatico **di** tutti i tuoi amici. *He's the most pleasant of all your friends.*
Lui è **il meno** simpatico **di** tutti i tuoi amici. *He's the least pleasant of all your friends.*
Lui è simpatic**issimo**/**molto simpatico.** *He's very pleasant.*

☞ The relative superlative is formed by placing the definite article before **più** or **meno**.
Sometimes the prepositions **tra** or **fra** may be found instead of **di**:
È la **più** simpatica **fra** tutti. *She's the most pleasant of all.*

☞ • The absolute superlative is usually formed by adding -**issimo/a/e/i** to the root of the adjective
or by placing adverbs of quantity (**molto, tanto, assai** , ... = very) in front of the adjective:
Loro sono **molto** simpatici = sono simpatic**issimi.**
• The absolute superlative is also formed by means of a prefix (**arci-, stra-, sopra-, super-, pluri-, ultra-**) or by repeating the adjective:
Arcinoto (very well known); **stra**ricco (extremely rich).
È una camera piccola piccola. *It's a very small room.*
• There are also many idiomatic forms of the absolute superlative:
Stanco morto (dead tired); ubriaco fradicio (as drunk as a lord); pieno zeppo (packed full); ricco sfondato (rolling in wealth); innamorato cotto (infatuated).

3.22 Irregular Comparison

Some adjectives have two comparative forms (the irregular one derives from the Latin):
Questa pizza è buonissima = questa pizza è ottima. *This pizza is excellent/very good.*

	COMPARATIVE	RELATIVE SUPERLATIVE	ABSOLUTE SUPERLATIVE
buono *(good)*	più buono/**migliore** *(better)*	il più buono/**il migliore** *(the best)*	buonissimo/**ottimo** *(very good)*
cattivo *(bad)*	più cattivo/**peggiore** *(worse)*	il più cattivo/**il peggiore** *(the worst)*	cattivissimo/**pessimo** *(very bad)*
grande *(big)*	più grande/**maggiore** *(bigger)*	il più grande/**il maggiore** *(the biggest)*	grandissimo/**massimo** *(very big)*
piccolo *(small)*	più piccolo/**minore** *(smaller)*	il più piccolo/**il minore** *(the smallest)*	piccolissimo/**minimo** *(very small)*
alto *(high)*	più alto/**superiore** *(higher)*	il più alto/**il superiore** *(the highest)*	altissimo/**supremo** *(very high)*
basso *(low)*	più basso/**inferiore** *(lower)*	il più basso/**l'inferiore** *(the lowest)*	bassissimo/**infimo** *(very low)*

4. ADVERBS (AVVERBI)

The adverb is the word that specifies the meaning of a verb, an adjective or another adverb.

e.g. Può parlare **lentamente**? *Can you speak slowly?*
È un ragazzo **molto** intelligente. *He's a very intelligent boy.*
Parli troppo **velocement**e! *You speak too quickly!*

4.1 Formation of Adverbs

In general

☞ Most adverbs (indicating manner) are derived by adding the suffix -**mente**:
  • to the feminine singular of adjectives in -**o**:
    Lento-lentamente (slowly), libero-liberamente (freely).
  • to the singular of adjectives in -**e**:
    Veloce-velocemente (quickly), breve-brevemente (briefly).
  • to adjectives in -**le/-re** (leaving out the -**e**):
    Facile-facilmente (easily), regolare-regolarmente (regularly).

☞ There are also adverbs (indicating quantity) that have a form identical to that of a few masculine singular adjectives: **troppo** (too; too much), **molto** [(very) much; a lot)], **tanto** (so; so much), **poco** (little; not much), ...

☞ Finally there are adverbs (indicating place or time) that have a form not derived from other words: **qui/qua** (here), **lì/là** (there), **mai** (never), **adesso** (now), **dove** (where), ...

4.2 Position of Adverbs

They are usually placed:

• after the verb: Puoi ripetere **chiaramente**? *Can you repeat clearly?*
• before the adjective: **Lei** è **molto** simpatica. *She's very nice.*
• between the auxiliary and the verb in compound tenses: È **già** partito. *He's already left.*

4.3 Classes of Adverbs

• **Manner** (answering the question 'how?'):
  facilmente, lentamente, raramente (rarely), ...
• **Place** (answering the question 'where?'):
  qui, lì, laggiù (down there), sotto (below), sopra (above), ...
• **Time** (answering the question 'when?'):
  adesso (now), oggi (today), domani (tomorrow), prima (before), dopo (after), ...
• **Quantity** (answering the question 'how much?'):
  molto, poco, troppo, abbastanza (enough), ...

Continued

4.4 Adverbial Phrases

In Italian, it is quite common to find expressions formed from two or more words, acquiring the meaning of an adverb.

e.g. **All'improvviso** (suddenly, **poco fa** (a little while ago), **nel frattempo** (in the meantime), **d'ora in poi** (from now on), **poco per volta** (a little at a time).

4.5 Comparison of Adverbs

☞ Some adverbs (mainly those of manner and a few of time and place) can be made into comparatives and superlatives (see 3.20, 3.21): lentamente, più lentamente, lentissimamente (slowly, more slowly, very slowly).

4.6 Irregular Forms

	COMPARATIVE	SUPERLATIVE
bene *well*	meglio *better*	benissimo/ottimamente *very well*
male *badly*	peggio *worse*	malissimo/pessimamente *very badly*
poco *little*	meno *less*	pochissimo *very little*
molto *very; a lot*	più *more*	moltissimo *very much*

Note

- *The adverb is invariable: lei legge molto. (She reads a lot); lui è molto simpatico (He's very nice); loro sono molto simpatici (They are very nice).*

- *Qui, qua = here ; lì, là = there. Qui and lì indicate a more precise location than qua and là.*

5. PERSONAL PRONOUNS (PRONOMI PERSONALI)

	SUBJECT	DIRECT OBJECT		INDIRECT OBJECT	
		stressed	unstressed	stressed	unstressed
I	**Io** invito	invitano **me**	**mi** invitano	spediscono a **me**	**mi** spediscono
you	**tu**	**te**	**ti**	**te**	**ti**
he; it	**egli (lui); esso**	**lui**	**lo**	**lui**	**gli**
she; it	**ella (lei); essa**	**lei**	**la**	**lei**	**le**
we	**noi**	**noi**	**ci**	**noi**	**ci**
you	**voi**	**voi**	**vi**	**voi**	**vi**
they	**essi (loro)**	**loro**	**li**	**loro**	**gli**
they	**esse (loro)**	**loro**	**le**	**loro**	**gli**

e.g. **Io** invito Emilio e Lisa. *I'm inviting Emilio and Lisa.*   - subject
Invitano **me**. *They're inviting me.*   - stressed direct object
Mi invitano. *They're inviting me.*   - unstressed direct object
Spediscono un libro a **me**. *They send a book to me.*   - stressed indirect object
Mi spediscono un libro. *They send a book to me.*   - unstressed indirect object

5.1 Subject:

Io (I); **tu** (you 'informal'), **Lei** (you 'formal'); **egli/lui** (he); **ella, lei** (she); **esso, essa** (it);
noi (we); **voi** (you); **essi, esse, loro** (they).

* The personal pronoun is normally used for the subject when it is necessary to emphasise who is carrying out an action.
  e.g. Vado al mercato. *I'm going to the market.*
       Io vado al mercato, tu resti a casa. *I'm going to the market, you stay at home.*
* In the polite form of address when talking to a person (man or woman) with whom one is not on familiar terms, **Lei** is used followed by the verb in the third person singular.
  e.g. Tu parli italiano? *Do you speak Italian?* - informal
       Lei parla italiano? *Do you speak Italian?* - formal
* **Egli, ella** usually refer to people and are often substituted by **lui, lei.**
* **Ella** is almost never used. It can be found in literature or bureaucratic language.
* **Esso, essa** refer mainly to objects or animals and are often substituted by **lui, lei.**
* **Essi, esse** refer to people, animals or objects and are often substituted by **loro.**

5.2 Stressed/unstressed direct object and stressed indirect object:

me, mi (me); **te, ti** (you 'informal'); **La** (you 'formal'); **lui, lo** (him); **lei, la** (her); **lo, la** (it);
noi, ci (us); **voi, vi** (you); **essi, esse, loro, li, le** (them).

5.3 Unstressed indirect object:

mi (to me); **ti** (to you 'informal'); **Le** (to you 'formal'); **gli** (to him); **le** (to her);
ci (to us); **vi** (to you); **gli** (to them).

* **Gli** more and more often substitutes **loro,** which is used mainly in formal situations and in the written language.
  e.g. Gli spediscono i libri = Spediscono loro i libri. *They send the books to them.*

Continued ➡

5.4 Use and Position of Personal Pronouns

☞ **Stressed forms** (which emphasize the pronoun) generally follow the verb and are used:
• for the direct object: Invitano me.
• for the indirect object, preceded by a preposition: Spediscono un libro a me.
• in comparison: È più giovane di lei. *He's younger than she.*
• in exclamations without a verb: Povero me! *Dear me!*

☞ **Unstressed forms**, (which emphasize the verb), generally precede the verb and are used:
• for the direct object: Mi invitano.
• for the indirect object, without a preposition: Mi spediscono un libro.

☞ **Unstressed** (or conjunctive) personal pronouns follow the verb to make, with the exception of **loro**, one single word:
• with the infinitive: Vengo a prenderti. *I'll come to get you.*
• with the gerund: Scrivendogli ha risolto il problema. *Writing to him solved the problem.*
• with the imperative: Telefonagli subito!'*Phone him at once!*; Telefona loro! '*Phone them!*
• with the past participle: Consegnatagli la lettera, uscì. *After handing him the letter, he left.*

☞ **Unstressed personal pronouns** follow the adverb **ecco** to make one single word (eccolo, eccola, eccoli, eccole, ...): Dov'è il libro? **Eccolo**. *Where is the book? Here it is.*

5.5 Personal Pronouns and the Apostrophe

In front of a vowel the pronouns:
• **lo** and **la** generally take an apostrophe: Non l'ho visto. *I haven't seen him;*
• **mi, ti, ci, vi** may take an apostrophe:
  M'ha già detto che non verrà = Mi ha già detto che non verrà.
  He has already told me that he won't be coming.

5.6 Personal Pronouns and the Past Participle

When the past participle is accompanied by the verb **avere**, it must agree with the direct object pronouns: **lo, la, li, le.**

e.g.

(libro)	L'ho comprato in Italia.	*I bought it in Italy.*
(penna)	L'ho comprata in Francia.	*I bought it in France.*
(libri)	Li ho comprati in Svizzera.	*I bought them in Switzerland.*
(penne)	Le ho comprate in Austria.	*I bought them in Austria.*

5.7 Combined Pronouns

• When necessary, the unstressed pronouns can be combined; in this case direct object pronouns follow the indirect object pronoun.
• **Mi, ti, ci, vi** change to **me, te, ce, ve** when followed by **lo, la, li, le, ne**:
  (Io) Ti spedisco il libro = **Te lo** spedisco. *I'll send it to you.*
  (tu) Mi spedisci le fotografie = **Me le** spedisci. *You'll send them to me.*
  Ve ne impresto due. *I'm going to lend you two of these.*
• **Gli** and **le** change to **glie-**, when followed by **lo, la, li, le, ne (glielo, gliela, glieli, gliele, gliene)**: Glielo dirò domani. *I'll tell it to him/her/them tomorrow.*
  to him it

che	who, whom, which, that
cui	whom, which
il quale (la quale, i quali, le quali)	who, whom, which, that
chi	he who, him who...

5.9 Che is invariable and can:

- only be used as subject or direct object;
- be substituted by **il quale, la quale, i quali, le quali**:
  Ho conosciuto un ragazzo che (= il quale) abita a Varese. *I met a boy who lives in Varese.*
  Ho conosciuto una ragazza che (=la quale) abita a Milano. *I met a girl who lives in Milan.*
  Le ragazze che (=le quali) hai conosciuto sono inglesi. *The girls that you met are English.*
  La torta che abbiamo mangiato, era molto buona. *The cake we ate was very nice.*

5.10 Cui is invariable and can:

- be used as indirect object (preceded by a preposition):
  Ecco il libro di cui ti ho parlato. *Here's the book I told you about.*
- be substituted by **il quale, la quale, i quali, le quali** in indirect object (preceded by a preposition+the definite article): Ecco il libro del quale ti ho parlato.
- be preceded by the definite article (**il cui, la cui**, ...= whose):
  Quel ragazzo, il cui nome non ricordo, è italiano.
  That boy, whose name I don't remember, is Italian.

5.11 Il quale is variable and is used:

- as subject (more formal than **che**):
  I ragazzi i quali (=che) vinceranno la competizione andranno in Italia.
  The boys who win the competition will go to Italy.
- rarely as direct object:
  Le ragazze le quali (=che) hai conosciuto sono inglesi. *The girls that you met are English.*
- quite frequently as indirect object (preceded by a preposition+the definite article):
  Il treno con il quale (= con cui) ho viaggiato era molto veloce.
  The train by which I travelled was very fast.

5.12 Chi is invariable and is only used in the singular. It refers to people. It is equivalent to
colui che (he who), **colei che** (she who), **la persona che** (the person who),
coloro che (they who, those who, ...):
Chi ha già il biglietto può entrare. *Whoever has got a ticket can go in.*
Coloro che hanno già il biglietto possono entrare. *Those with a ticket can go in.*

5.13 INTERROGATIVE PRONOUNS (PRONOMI INTERROGATIVI)

chi ?	who?
che (cosa)?	what?
quale ?	which?
quanto ?	how much?

e.g. **Chi** ha telefonato? *Who 'phoned?*
Che cosa hai detto? *What did you say?*
Quale dei due preferisci? *Which of these two do you prefer?*
Quanto costa? *How much is it?*

5.14 Chi? is invariable and is used for people or animals:

Chi non ha mangiato il dolce? *Who hasn't eaten the cake?*
Chi ha rotto il vaso? *Who broke the vase?*

5.15 Che? is invariable and is used for objects (it is equivalent to **che cosa**? or **cosa**?):

Che (cosa) avete comprato? *What did you buy?*
(Che) cosa vuoi fare? *What would you like to do?*

5.16 Quale? varies in the plural (**quali**) and is used for people, animals or objects:

Quale di questi vestiti compreresti? *Which of these dresses would you buy?*
Di queste parole quali conosci? *Which of these words do you know?*

5.17 Quanto? is variable (**quanto, quanta, quanti, quante**) and is used for people, animals or objects:

Quanto le devo? *How much do I owe you?*
Quanta ne desidera? *How much would you like?*
Quanti verranno alla tua festa? *How many are coming to your party?*
Quante sono venute alla tua festa? *How many came to your party?*

5.18 DEMONSTRATIVE PRONOUNS (PRONOMI DIMOSTRATIVI)

5.19 (this, that) questo, quello, ...

	SINGULAR	PLURAL	
MASCULINE	questo quello	questi quelli	this; these that; those
FEMININE	questa quella	queste quelle	

e.g. Preferisco questa spiaggia perché **quella** è troppo affollata.
I prefer this beach because that one is too crowded.
Queste maglie sono di cotone e **quelle** sono di lana. *These vests are cotton and those are woollen.*
Questi occhiali sono molto più cari di **quelli**. *These spectacles are much dearer than those.*
Questo è un ottimo ristorante. *This is an excellent restaurant.*

- *The most used demonstrative pronouns have a form similar to that of demonstrative adjectives with the exception of **quelli** (see 3.7).*
- *Remember that pronouns substitute a noun , while adjectives accompany a noun.*

5.20 **Questi** (this man; the latter), **quegli** (that man; the former) are only used:
- in the masculine singular;
- as subject:
  Siamo andati al mare con Louis e John: **quegli** è francese, **questi** è inglese.
  We went to the seaside with Louis and John: the former is French, the latter is English.

5.21 **Costui** (this man; he; him;), **costei** (this woman; she; her;), **colui** (that man...), **colei** (that woman...); **costoro** (these people; they; them); **coloro** (those people; they; them) can be used:
- in a disparaging manner;
- as subject or object:
  Chi è **costui**? *Who's this man?*
  Non voglio più vedere **costei**. *I don't want to see this woman any more.*
  Costui è un disonesto. *This man is a rogue.*

- *The demonstrative pronouns **questi, quegli, costui, costei, costoro, colui, colei** and **coloro** are generally formal and seldom used.*

18

5.22 Indefinite Pronouns (Pronomi Indefiniti)

5.23 (one, someone, ...) uno, qualcuno, ...

SINGULAR

MASCULINE	**uno**	one, someone
	qualcuno	somebody, someone, anybody, anyone
	ognuno	everybody, everyone
	chiunque	anybody, anyone
	qualcosa/qualche cosa	something, anything
	niente/nulla	nothing, anything
FEMININE	**una**	
	qualcuna	
	ognuna	
	chiunque	
	-	
	-	

e.g. C'è **uno** che ti cerca. *Someone is looking for you.*
Ha telefonato **qualcuno**? *Has anyone 'phoned?*
Ognuno ha ricevuto un regalo. *Everyone received a present.*
Può entrare **chiunque**. *Anyone can come in.*
C'è **qualcosa** che non funziona. *There's something that doesn't work.*
Non è **niente**, non ti preoccupare. *It's nothing, don't worry.*
Vi serve **nulla**? *Do you need anything?*

5.24 (everyone, nobody, ...) ciascuno, nessuno, ...

Other indefinite pronouns are similar, in both form and use,
to indefinite adjectives (see 3.12, 3.13, 3.14). Among these are:

- **ciascuno**, ciascuna (*everyone, everybody, each, each one*)
  nessuno, nessuna (*nobody, no-one*)
- **altro**, altra, altri, altre (*another, others*)
  molto, molta, molte, molti (*a lot, many*)
  parecchio, parecchia, parecchi, parecchie (*quite a lot, several*)
  poco, poca, pochi, poche (*a little, not much, few*)
  tanto, tanta ,tanti, tante (*a lot, many*)
  troppo, troppa, troppi, troppe (*too much, too many*)
  tutto, tutta, tutti, tutte (*all, everything, everybody*)
- **alcuno**, alcuna, alcuni, alcune (*anybody, anyone, some, a few*)

e.g. **Ciascuno** deve fare i compiti. *Everyone has to do his homework.*
Nessuna è più simpatica di Piera. *No one is nicer than Piera.*
Qualcuno ha fatto il bagno, **altri** hanno preso il sole. *Some had a swim, others sunbathed.*
Ha molti dischi, **alcuni** sono di musica classica. *He's got a lot of records, some are classical music.*
Vuoi **altro**? *Do you want anything else?*

5.25 POSSESSIVE PRONOUNS (PRONOMI POSSESSIVI)

	MASCULINE			FEMININE		
	SINGULAR	PLURAL		SINGULAR	PLURAL	
(il)	mio	(i) miei	(la)	mia	(le) mie	(mine)
	tuo	tuoi		tua	tue	(yours) 'informal'
	Suo	Suoi		Sua	Sue	(yours) 'formal'
	suo	suoi		sua	sue	(his, hers)
	nostro	nostri		nostra	nostre	(ours)
	vostro	vostri		vostra	vostre	(yours)
	loro	loro		loro	loro	(theirs)

e.g.   Non trovo la mia penna, mi presti la **tua**? *I can't find my pen, will you lend me yours?*
Suo padre è inglese, **il mio** è italiano. *His father is English, mine is Italian.*

Note

- *Possessive adjectives and pronouns have identical forms (see 3.8)*
- *Possessive pronouns agree with the implied object.*
- *Possessive pronouns are almost always preceded by the article.*
- ***I miei** and **i tuoi** can also indicate "my/your parents" or more generally "my/your family":*
  Vado in Italia con i miei. (I'm going to Italy with my family.)
- *To make a toast one can also say "**alla** + the possessive feminine singular":*
  Alla nostra (salute) [To our health!]. Alla tua! (To your health!)
- *Possessive pronouns in the feminine singular are often used in commercial and, less frequently, private correspondence:*
  Con riferimento alla Vostra del 24... (Referring to your letter of 24th...)
  Oggi ho ricevuto la tua... (Today I received your letter...)
- *The most common abbreviations of possessive adjectives and pronouns in commercial correspondence are:*
  s., S., (suo, Suo - your); V. (vostro, vostra - your); Vs (Vostra lettera - your letter); ns. (nostro -our).

6. COMMON USES OF SI - CI - VI - NE

6.1 Si

Reflexive
- **Si** (himself, herself, itself, themselves, oneself): Si lavano. *They wash themselves.*
- **Si** (his, her, their): Si lava le mani. *He washes his hands.*
- **Si** (each other; one another):
  Si scrivono una volta al mese. *They write to each other once a month.*

Impersonal
- Si (one; you; we; they; people) + 'verb' in the third person singular:
  Si dice che sia molto ambizioso. *People say he's very ambitious.*

Passive
- **Si** + 'verb' in the third person singular and plural:
  Si vende il vino novello. *The new wine is on sale.*
  Non si fanno sconti. *No discounts given.*

- *The reflexive unstressed pronoun **si** (= **sé** stressed) is used in the third person singular and plural.*
  *Sé can be emphasized by **stesso -a -i -e:** Pensano solo a sé stessi. (They think only of themselves.)*
- *Si changes to **se** when it is followed by **lo, la, li, le** or **ne.***
- *Si can take an apostrophe in front of a vowel: S'è fatto male. (He hurt himself.)*
- *Sì = yes.*
- *Se (conjunction) = if, whether.*

6.2 Ci and Vi

Personal Pronouns
- **Ci** (=noi) , **vi** (=voi): Ci invita. Vi saluta. *He invites us. He greets you.*
- **Ci** (=a noi), **vi** (=a voi): Ci presta il libro. Vi scrive. *He lends the book to us. He writes to you.*

Demonstrative Pronoun
- **Ci** = a ciò, di ciò, in ciò, su ciò, da ciò. (to it/this/that/, about it, ...):
  Pensaci! *Think about it!*
  Non ci fare caso. *Don't bother.*

Adverbs of Place
- **Ci/vi** = qua, là (here, there):
  Ci (=qua) venite tutti gli anni? *Do you come here every year?*
  Vi (=qua) resteremo due settimane. *We'll stay here two weeks.*
  C'è; c'era; ci sono, ... *There is; there was; there are, ...*

- *Ci and vi take an apostrophe only in front of the vowels **e** and, less frequently, **i**:*
  C'è la doccia. C'indica la strada. (There is a shower. He shows us the way.)
- *Vi, as an adverb of place, is seldom used in colloquial Italian.*

6.3 Ne

Pronoun
- **Ne** (of him/her/them): Non ne (=di lui) parli mai. *You never talk about him.*
  Ne (=di loro) parla sempre male. *He always talks badly of them.*
- **Ne** (by him/her/them): Ne (=da lui) rimase impressionato. *He was impressed by him.*
- **Ne** (of this/that...): Quanto ne (=di questo) vuoi? *How much do you want (of this)?*
  Ne abbiamo due. *We have two (of these).* Che cosa ne pensate? *What do you think (of this/that)?*

Adverb
- **Ne** (from here/there): Me ne vado. Ne uscì subito. *I'm going from here. He went out immediately.*

- *Ne can take an apostrophe: Non se n'era accorto. (He hadn't realized.) Me n'andai via. (I left.)*
- *Né ... **né** = neither... nor; either... or.*

Moods	Simple Tenses	e.g.		Compound Tenses	e.g.	
INDICATIVE	present	**abito**	I live, I am living, I do live	perfect	**ho abitato**	I have lived
	imperfect	**abitavo**	I was living, I used to live, I lived	pluperfect	**avevo abitato**	I had lived
	past historic	**abitai**	I lived	past anterior	**ebbi abitato**	I had lived
	future	**abiterò**	I'll live, I am going to live	future perfect	**avrò abitato**	I'll have lived
SUBJUNCTIVE	present	**abiti**	I live	perfect	**abbia abitato**	I have lived
	imperfect	**abitassi**	I lived	pluperfect	**avessi abitato**	I had lived
CONDITIONAL	present	**abiterei**	I'd live	perfect	**avrei abitato**	I'd have lived
IMPERATIVE	present	**abita!**	live!			
PARTICIPLE	present	**abitante**	living			
	past	**abitato**	lived			
GERUND	present	**abitando**	living	past	**avendo abitato**	having lived
INFINITIVE	present	**abitare**	to live	perfect	**avere abitato**	to have lived

☞ Italian verbs are divided into three groups according to the ending of the infinitive:
verbs ending in **-are** (*abitare, parlare, guardare, ...*)
verbs ending in **-ere** (*ripetere, vivere, leggere, ...*)
verbs ending in **-ire** (*partire, aprire, preferire, ...*)

Note

The English equivalents of the Italian verb tenses set out above are only given as simple examples since, in some cases, an Italian tense corresponds to a different one in English. For full explanations of tense translation refer to the relevant grammar sheet.

	ESSERE *to be*	AVERE *to have*	ABITARE *to live*	RIPETERE *to repeat*	PARTIRE *to leave*
I	sono	ho	abit**o**	ripet**o**	part**o**
you	sei	hai	abit**i**	ripet**i**	part**i**
he, she, it	è	ha	abit**a**	ripet**e**	part**e**
we	siamo	abbiamo	abit**iamo**	ripet**iamo**	part**iamo**
you	siete	avete	abit**ate**	ripet**ete**	part**ite**
they	sono	hanno	abit**ano**	ripet**ono**	part**ono**

☞ The present tense is used:
- when the action takes place at the time the subject speaks:
  Compro il giornale. *I'm buying the newspaper.*
- to render an action that is habitual:
  Il telegiornale **inizia** alle 20.30. *The news starts at 20:30.*
- often in proverbs:
  Chi **cerca trova**. *Seek and you will find.*
- instead of the past tense to make a narrative more vivid:
  C. Colombo **parte** da Palos nel 1492 ... *In 1492 C. Columbus sailed from Palos ...*

Irregular Verbs

☞
- Many verbs of the third conjugation (**-IRE**) insert **-isc-** between the stem and the ending in the singular and in the third person plural.
  Some of the most common are: capire (to understand); finire (to finish); preferire (to prefer); spedire (to send); suggerire (to suggest); ubbidire (to obey).

e.g.	CAPIRE	FINIRE
	cap-isc-o	fin-isc-o
	cap-isc-i	fin-isc-i
	cap-isc-e	fin-isc-e
	capiamo	finiamo
	capite	finite
	cap-isc-ono	fin-isc-ono

☞
- Verbs ending in **-ciare** and **-giare** lose the **i** in front of an **i** .
- Verbs ending in **-care** and **-gare** take an **h** in front of an **i**.

e.g.	PRONUNCIARE *to pronounce*	VIAGGIARE *to travel*	CERCARE *to look for*	PAGARE *to pay*
	pronuncio	viaggio	cerco	pago
	pronunci	viagg**i**	cerc**h**i	pag**h**i
	pronuncia	viaggia	cerca	paga
	pronunciamo	viaggiamo	cerc**h**iamo	pag**h**iamo
	pronunciate	viaggiate	cercate	pagate
	pronunciano	viaggiano	cercano	pagano

Continued ➡

Common Irregular Verbs

☞	ANDARE	*to go*	vado, vai, va; andiamo, andate, vanno.
	BERE	*to drink*	bevo, bevi, beve; beviamo, bevete, bevono.
	DARE	*to give*	do, dai, dà; diamo, date, danno.
	DIRE	*to say, to tell*	dico, dici, dice; diciamo, dite, dicono.
	FARE	*to make, to do*	faccio, fai, fa; facciamo, fate, fanno.
	PIACERE	*to like*	piaccio, piaci, piace; piacciamo, piacete, piacciono.
	RIMANERE	*to remain*	rimango, rimani, rimane; rimaniamo, rimanete, rimangono.
	SALIRE	*to go up*	salgo, sali, sale; saliamo, salite, salgono.
	SAPERE	*to know*	so, sai, sa; sappiamo, sapete, sanno.
	SCEGLIERE	*to choose*	scelgo, scegli, sceglie; scegliamo, scegliete, scelgono.
	STARE	*to stay*	sto, stai, sta; stiamo, state, stanno.
	TRADURRE	*to translate*	traduco, traduci, traduce; traduciamo, traducete, traducono.
	USCIRE	*to go out*	esco, esci, esce; usciamo, uscite, escono.
	VENIRE	*to come*	vengo, vieni, viene; veniamo, venite, vengono.
	DOVERE	*to have to*	devo, devi, deve; dobbiamo, dovete, devono.
	POTERE	*to be able*	posso, puoi, può; possiamo, potete, possono.
	VOLERE	*to want*	voglio, vuoi, vuole; vogliamo, volete, vogliono.

7.2. IMPERFECT INDICATIVE (IMPERFETTO INDICATIVO)

Regular verbs

	ESSERE	AVERE	ABITARE	RIPETERE	PARTIRE
I	ero	avevo	abit**avo**	ripet**evo**	part**ivo**
you	eri	avevi	abit**avi**	ripet**evi**	part**ivi**
he,she,it	era	aveva	abit**ava**	ripet**eva**	part**iva**
we	eravamo	avevamo	abit**avamo**	ripet**evamo**	part**ivamo**
you	eravate	avevate	abit**avate**	ripet**evate**	part**ivate**
they	erano	avevano	abit**avano**	ripet**evano**	part**ivano**

☞ The imperfect is used to express:
- indeterminate duration of an action in the past:
  Alle dieci **studiavo** ancora. *At ten o'clock I was still studying.*
- continuity and repetition of an action in the past:
  Tutte le sere **guardavo** la televisione. *Every evening I used to watch TV.*
- two contemporaneous actions in the past:
  Mentre **scrivevo**, lui **ascoltava** la musica. *While I was writing, he was listening to music.*

Common Irregular Verbs

BERE	*to drink*	bevevo, bevevi, beveva; bevevamo, bevevate, bevevano.
DIRE	*to say, to tell*	dicevo, dicevi, diceva; dicevamo, dicevate, dicevano.
FARE	*to make, to do*	facevo, facevi, faceva; facevamo, facevate, facevano.
TRADURRE	*to translate*	traducevo, traducevi, traduceva; traducevamo, traducevate, traducevano.

7.3 PLUPERFECT (TRAPASSATO PROSSIMO)

	ESSERE	AVERE	ABITARE	RIPETERE	PARTIRE
	ero stato/a	avevo avuto	avevo abit**ato**	avevo ripet**uto**	ero partito/a
	eri stato/a	avevi avuto	avevi abitato	avevi ripetuto	eri partito/a
	era stato/a	aveva avuto	aveva abitato	aveva ripetuto	era partito/a
	eravamo stati/e	avevamo avuto	avevamo abitato	avevamo ripetuto	eravamo partiti/e
	eravate stati/e	avevate avuto	avevate abitato	avevate ripetuto	eravate partiti/e
	erano stati/e	avevano avuto	avevano abitato	avevano ripetuto	erano partiti/e

☞ The pluperfect is used to express:

- a past action that happened before another action, also in the past:
  Era appena uscito, quando telefonò Enrica. *He had just gone out, when Enrica 'phoned.*

☞ The pluperfect is formed:

- from the imperfect of **avere** or **essere** followed by the past participle of the verb (see 7.5).

7.4 PERFECT INDICATIVE (PASSATO PROSSIMO)

ESSERE	AVERE	ABITARE	RIPETERE	PARTIRE
sono stato/a	ho avuto	ho abit**ato**	ho ripet**uto**	sono part**ito/a**
sei stato/a	hai avuto	hai abitato	hai ripetuto	sei partito/a
è stato/a	ha avuto	ha abitato	ha ripetuto	è partito/a
siamo stati/e	abbiamo avuto	abbiamo abitato	abbiamo ripetuto	siamo partiti/e
siete stati/e	avete avuto	avete abitato	avete ripetuto	siete partiti/e
sono stati/e	hanno avuto	hanno abitato	hanno ripetuto	sono partiti/e

☞ It is used to indicate:
  - an action that happened in a past that has not yet completely ended or has just ended:
    Quest'anno sono andato in Italia. *This year I've been to Italy.*
  - an action in the past the effects of which are still continuing:
    C. Colombo ha scoperto l'America. *C. Columbus discovered America.*

☞ The perfect is formed from the present of **avere** or **essere** and the past participle of the verb.

☞ The past participle agrees with the subject when it is preceded by the auxiliary **essere:**
Maria è partita. Giorgio è partito. Maria e Rosa sono partite.
Maria has left. Giorgio has left. Maria and Rosa have left.
Giorgio e Antonio sono partiti. Maria e Giorgio sono partiti.
Giorgio and Antonio have left. Maria and Giorgio have left.

☞ The most common verbs that take the auxiliary **essere** are:
partire, arrivare, andare, venire, tornare, entrare, uscire, salire, scendere, stare, rimanere, piacere, riuscire, diventare.

7.5 PAST PARTICIPLE (PARTICIPIO PASSATO)

ESSERE	AVERE	ABITARE	RIPETERE	PARTIRE
stato/a/i/e	avuto	abit**ATO**	ripet**UTO**	part**ITO**

Common Irregular Verbs

ACCENDERE *to turn on*	acceso		DIRE *to tell, to say*	detto
CHIUDERE *to close*	chiuso		FARE *to make, to do*	fatto
CORRERE *to run*	corso		LEGGERE *to read*	letto
DECIDERE *to decide*	deciso		SCRIVERE *to write*	scritto
METTERE *to put*	messo			
PRENDERE *to take*	preso		APRIRE *to open*	aperto
PROMETTERE *to promise*	promesso		OFFRIRE *to offer*	offerto
TRASCORRERE *to spend*	trascorso		SCEGLIERE *to choose*	scelto
			SPEGNERE *to turn off*	spento
CHIEDERE *to ask*	chiesto			
RISPONDERE *to reply*	risposto		BERE *to drink*	bevuto

ESSERE *to be*	stato/a/i/e
NASCERE *to be born*	nato/a/i/e
RIMANERE *to remain*	rimasto/a/i/e
VENIRE *to come*	venuto/a/i/e
SCENDERE *to come down*	sceso/a/i/e

7.6 FUTURE (FUTURO)

ESSERE	AVERE		ABITARE	RIPETERE	PARTIRE
sarò	avrò		abiterò	ripeterò	partirò
sarai	avrai		abiterai	ripeterai	partirai
sarà	avrà		abiterà	ripeterà	partirà
saremo	avremo		abiteremo	ripeteremo	partiremo
sarete	avrete		abiterete	ripeterete	partirete
saranno	avranno		abiteranno	ripeteranno	partiranno

☞ The future is used to indicate:
- an action that is still to come, with respect to the time in which one is talking:
  Domani **partirò** per l'Italia. *Tomorrow I'm leaving for Italy.*
- a doubt, a hypothesis:
  Avrà quindici anni. *He may be fifteen.*
- an order, referring to the future:
  Resterai a casa con tua sorella! *You'll stay at home with your sister!*

> **Note** *The present indicative is often used in spoken language to indicate an action that is still to happen: Domani parto per l'Italia. Tomorrow I'm leaving for Italy.*

Common Irregular Verbs

☞ Verbs ending in **-ciare** and **-giare** lose the i in front of an **e**.

e.g. **COMINCIARE** *to start*   comincerò, comincerai, comincerà; cominceremo, comincerete, cominceranno.
    VIAGGIARE *to travel*   viaggerò, viaggerai, viaggerà; viaggeremo, viaggerete, viaggeranno.

☞ Verbs ending in **-care** and **-gare** take an **h** in front of an **e**.

e.g. **CERCARE** *to look for*   cercherò, cercherai, cercherà; cercheremo, cercherete, cercheranno.
    PAGARE *to pay*   pagherò, pagherai, pagherà; pagheremo, pagherete, pagheranno.

☞
ANDARE	*to go*	andrò, andrai, andrà; andremo, andrete, andranno.
DOVERE	*to have to*	dovrò, dovrai, dovrà; dovremo, dovrete, dovranno.
POTERE	*to be able*	potrò, potrai, potrà; potremo, potrete, potranno.
SAPERE	*to know*	saprò, saprai, saprà; sapremo, saprete, sapranno.
VEDERE	*to see*	vedrò, vedrai, vedrà; vedremo, vedrete, vedranno.
VIVERE	*to live*	vivrò, vivrai, vivrà; vivremo, vivrete, vivranno.

☞
BERE	*to drink*	berrò, berrai, berrà; berremo, berrete, berranno.
RIMANERE	*to remain*	rimarrò, rimarrai, rimarrà; rimarremo, rimarrete, rimarranno.
TRADURRE	*to translate*	tradurrò, tradurrai, tradurrà; tradurremo, tradurrete, tradurranno.
VENIRE	*to come*	verrò, verrai, verrà; verremo, verrete, verranno.
VOLERE	*to want*	vorrò, vorrai, vorrà; vorremo, vorrete, vorranno.

☞
DIRE	*to say*	dirò, dirai, dirà; diremo, direte, diranno.
FARE	*to make*	farò, farai, farà; faremo, farete, faranno.
STARE	*to stay*	starò, starai, starà; staremo, starete, staranno.

ESSERE	AVERE	ABITARE	RIPETERE	PARTIRE
sarò stato/a	avrò avuto	avrò abitato	avrò ripetuto	sarò partito/a
sarai stato/a	avrai avuto	avrai abitato	avrai ripetuto	sarai partito/a
sarà stato/a	avrà avuto	avrà abitato	avrà ripetuto	sarà partito/a
saremo stati/e	avremo avuto	avremo abitato	avremo ripetuto	saremo partiti/e
sarete stati/e	avrete avuto	avrete abitato	avrete ripetuto	sarete partiti/e
saranno stati/e	avranno avuto	avranno abitato	avranno ripetuto	saranno partiti/e

☞ The future perfect is normally used to indicate an action that will take place in the future but before another action also in the future:
Dopo che avrai mangiato, telefonerai a Renata. *After you've eaten, you'll 'phone Renata.*
Quando avrò finito i compiti, andrò al cinema. *When I have finished my homework, I'll go to the cinema.*

☞ The future perfect is formed from the simple future of **avere** or **essere** and the past participle of the verb.

28

7.8 PAST HISTORIC (PASSATO REMOTO)

ESSERE	AVERE		ABITARE	RIPETERE	PARTIRE
fui	ebbi		abita**i**	ripet**ei**	part**ii**
fosti	avesti		abita**sti**	ripet**esti**	part**isti**
fu	ebbe		abit**ò**	ripet**é**	part**ì**
fummo	avemmo		abit**ammo**	ripet**emmo**	part**immo**
foste	aveste		abit**aste**	ripet**este**	part**iste**
furono	ebbero		abit**arono**	ripet**erono**	part**irono**

☞ The past historic is used to indicate an action that happened in the past and which has completely ended, having no relation with the present:
Due anni fa andarono a Venezia. *Two years ago they went to Venice.*
L'anno scorso Nicola comprò una Ferrari. *Last year Nicola bought a Ferrari.*

- *Verbs in - ere can have the following forms in the first and third person singular and the third person plural respectively: -ei/-etti,-é/-ette,-erono/-ettero:*
Crederono di avere ragione = Credettero di avere ragione. (They thought they were right.)
- *The past historic is used mainly in written language. In spoken language it is more often replaced by the perfect indicative, especially in Northern Italy:*
L'anno scorso sono andata a Milano. (Last year I went to Milan.)

Common Irregular Verbs

BERE	*to drink*	bevvi, bevesti, bevve; bevemmo, beveste, bevvero.
CHIEDERE	*to ask*	chiesi, chiedesti, chiese; chiedemmo, chiedeste, chiesero.
CHIUDERE	*to close*	chiusi, chiudesti, chiuse; chiudemmo, chiudeste, chiusero.
CONOSCERE	*to know*	conobbi, conoscesti, conobbe; conoscemmo, conosceste, conobbero.
DARE	*to give*	diedi/detti, desti, diede/dette; demmo, deste , diedero/dettero.
DECIDERE	*to decide*	decisi, decidesti, decise; decidemmo, decideste, decisero.
DIRE	*to say, to tell*	dissi, dicesti, disse; dicemmo, diceste, dissero.
FARE	*to make, to do*	feci, facesti, fece; facemmo, faceste, fecero
LEGGERE	*to read*	lessi, leggesti, lesse; leggemmo, leggeste, lessero.
METTERE	*to put*	misi, mettesti, mise; mettemmo, metteste, misero.
NASCERE	*to be born*	nacqui, nascesti, nacque; nascemmo, nasceste, nacquero.
PERDERE	*to lose*	persi, perdesti, perse; perdemmo, perdeste, persero.
RIDERE	*to laugh*	risi, ridesti, rise; ridemmo, rideste, risero.
RIMANERE	*to remain*	rimasi, rimanesti, rimase; rimanemmo, rimaneste, rimasero.
RISPONDERE	*to reply*	risposi, rispondesti, rispose; rispondemmo, rispondeste, risposero.
SAPERE	*to know*	seppi, sapesti, seppe; sapemmo, sapeste, seppero.
SCEGLIERE	*to choose*	scelsi, scegliesti, scelse; scegliemmo, sceglieste, scelsero.
SCRIVERE	*to write*	scrissi, scrivesti, scrisse; scrivemmo, scriveste, scrissero.
STARE	*to stay*	stetti, stesti, stette; stemmo, steste, stettero.
TRADURRE	*to translate*	tradussi, traducesti ,tradusse; traducemmo, traduceste, tradussero.
VEDERE	*to see*	vidi,vedesti,vide; vedemmo, vedeste, videro.
VENIRE	*to come*	venni, venisti, venne; venimmo, veniste, vennero.
VINCERE	*to win*	vinsi, vincesti, vinse; vincemmo, vinceste, vinsero.
VIVERE	*to live*	vissi, vivesti, visse; vivemmo, viveste, vissero.
VOLERE	*to want*	volli, volesti, volle; volemmo, voleste, vollero.

- *Verbs in -ere are almost all irregular in the first and the third person singular and the third person plural.*

7.9 PRESENT CONDITIONAL (CONDIZIONALE PRESENTE)

ESSERE	AVERE	ABITARE	RIPETERE	PARTIRE
sarei	avrei	abiterei	ripeterei	partirei
saresti	avresti	abiteresti	ripeteresti	partiresti
sarebbe	avrebbe	abiterebbe	ripeterebbe	partirebbe
saremmo	avremmo	abiteremmo	ripeteremmo	partiremmo
sareste	avreste	abitereste	ripetereste	partireste
sarebbero	avrebbero	abiterebbero	ripeterebbero	partirebbero

☞ The present conditional is normally used:
- to indicate a possibility that will take place under certain conditions:
  Comprerei la frutta (se fosse fresca). *I would buy the fruit (if it were fresh).*
- in polite forms of address.
  Vorrei un biglietto di andata e ritorno per Pisa. *I'd like a return ticket to Pisa.*

☞ For the irregular forms see the future tense.
e.g. **Comincerei, andrei, dovrei, saprei, potrei, vedrei, vivrei, berrei,** etc.

7.10 PERFECT CONDITIONAL (CONDIZIONALE PASSATO)

ESSERE	AVERE	ABITARE	RIPETERE	PARTIRE
sarei stato/a	avrei avuto	avrei abitato	avrei ripetuto	sarei partito/a
saresti stato/a	avresti avuto	avresti abitato	avresti ripetuto	saresti partito/a
sarebbe stato/a	avrebbe avuto	avrebbe abitato	avrebbe ripetuto	sarebbe partito/a
saremmo stati/e	avremmo avuto	avremmo abitato	avremmo ripetuto	saremmo partiti/e
sareste stati/e	avreste avuto	avreste abitato	avreste ripetuto	sareste partiti/e
sarebbero stati/e	avrebbero avuto	avrebbero abitato	avrebbero ripetuto	sarebbero partiti/e

☞ The perfect conditional is normally used:
- to indicate a possibility that could have happened in the past under certain conditions:
  Avrei comprato la frutta (se fosse stata fresca). *I would have bought the fruit (if it had been fresh).*
- to express an action happening after another in the past:
  Hanno detto che **sarebbero andati** a Parigi. *They said they would go to Paris.*

☞ The perfect conditional is formed from the present conditional of **avere** or **essere** and the past participle of the verb.

7.11 PRESENT SUBJUNCTIVE (CONGIUNTIVO PRESENTE)

ESSERE	AVERE	ABITARE	RIPETERE	PARTIRE
sia	abbia	abiti	ripeta	parta
sia	abbia	abiti	ripeta	parta
sia	abbia	abiti	ripeta	parta
siamo	abbiamo	abit**iamo**	ripet**iamo**	part**iamo**
siate	abbiate	abit**iate**	ripet**iate**	part**iate**
siano	abbiano	abit**ino**	ripet**ano**	part**ano**

The subjunctive usually depends on another verb that indicates opinion, possibility, uncertainty, desire, ... [**credere** (to believe/think); **pensare** (to think/suppose); **sperare** (to hope), ...]

e.g. Penso che loro **abbiano** ragione. *I think they are right.*
Speriamo che il treno **sia** in orario. *Let's hope the train will be on time.*

In secondary clauses the subjunctive is always used after:
a condizione che (on condition that); affinché (so that); a meno che (unless); benché (although); nel caso che (in case); prima che (before). Bisogna che (it is necessary that); è meglio che (it is better that); è un peccato che (it is a pity that), ...

e.g. Telefonagli prima che **esca**. *'Phone him before he goes out.*
È un peccato che tu non **sia** qui con noi. *It's a pity you're not here with us.*

 In spoken language the subjunctive is often replaced by the indicative.

Common Irregular Verbs

ANDARE	*to go*	vada, vada, vada; andiamo, andiate, vadano.
BERE	*to drink*	beva, beva, beva; beviamo, beviate, bevano.
DARE	*to give*	dia, dia, dia; diamo, diate, diano.
DIRE	*to say, to tell*	dica, dica, dica; diciamo, diciate, dicano.
DOVERE	*to have to*	debba, debba, debba; dobbiamo, dobbiate, debbano.
FARE	*to make, to do*	faccia, faccia, faccia; facciamo, facciate, facciano.
POTERE	*to be able*	possa, possa, possa; possiamo, possiate, possano.
SCEGLIERE	*to choose*	scelga, scelga, scelga; scegliamo, scegliate, scelgano.
STARE	*to stay*	stia, stia, stia; stiamo, stiate, stiano.
TENERE	*to keep*	tenga, tenga, tenga; teniamo, teniate, tengano.
TRADURRE	*to translate*	traduca, traduca, traduca; traduciamo, traduciate, traducano.
USCIRE	*to go out*	esca, esca, esca; usciamo, usciate, escano.
VENIRE	*to come*	venga, venga, venga; veniamo, veniate, vengano.
VOLERE	*to want*	voglia, voglia, voglia; vogliamo, vogliate, vogliano.

7.12 IMPERATIVE (IMPERATIVO)

	ESSERE	AVERE	GIRARE	PRENDERE	PARTIRE
(tu)	sii	abbi	gira	prendi	parti
(Lei)	sia	abbia	giri	prenda	parta
(noi)	siamo	abbiamo	giriamo	prendiamo	partiamo
(voi)	siate	abbiate	girate	prendete	partite
(Loro)	siano	abbiano	girino	prendano	partano

☞ The imperative expresses a direct or indirect order, but also an exhortation, advice or a prayer.

Vieni subito qui! *Come here immediately!* **Giri** a destra! *Turn right!*

Non fate rumore ! *Don't make a noise!*

Studia, che domani ci sono gli esami! *Study, because you have exams tomorrow!*

Ascolta i consigli del medico: **mangia** meno dolci! *Listen to the doctor's advice: eat fewer sweets!*

- *The imperative does not have the first person singular **io**.*
- *With **tu,noi** and **voi** we use the imperative.*
- *With **Lei** and **Loro** we use the indirect imperative (=present subjunctive), which turns the order into an invitation.*
- *The future imperative = the future indicative: Verrai al mare!   (You will come to the seaside!)*

Negative imperative

- The negative imperative = non + imperative: (voi) Non girate a destra! *Don't turn right!*
- The imperative negative with the second singular person **tu** = non + infinitive:
  (tu) Non girare a destra! *Don't turn right!*

Imperative and pronouns

The imperative with unstressed pronouns, **ci** or **ne**, is usually formed
in the following ways:
- Imperative + pronouns (the verb and the pronouns form one word): Parlagli! Invitiamolo!
- Pronouns + indirect imperative (pronouns and verb are separate): Gli parli! Glielo scriva!

Negative imperative and pronouns.

- Non + imperative + pronouns: Non invitiamolo! Non scriveteglielo!
- Non + infinitive + pronouns (with the second person singular **tu**):
  Non parlargli! Non invitarlo!
- Non + pronouns + indirect imperative: Non gli parli! Non ce le spediscano!

Common Irregular Verbs

ANDARE *to go*	va', vada; andiamo, andate, vadano.
DARE *to give*	da', dia; diamo, date, diano.
DIRE *to say*	di', dica; diciamo, dite, dicano.
FARE *to make*	fa', faccia, facciamo, fate, facciano.
STARE *to stay*	sta', stia; stiamo, state, stiano.

- *Va' (=vai), da' (=dai), fa' (=fai), sta' (=stai)*
- *When **va', da', di', fa'** and **sta'** are followed by a personal pronoun (with the exception of **gli**), the consonant is doubled.*
  e.g. Valle a chiedere scusa! (Va' + le = valle). Dammi il mio libro! (Da' + mi = dammi).
  Fagli vedere le fotografie! (Fa' + gli = fagli).

7.13 GERUND (GERUNDIO)

	ESSERE	AVERE	ABITARE	RIPETERE	PARTIRE
Present	essendo	avendo	abit**ando**	ripet**endo**	part**endo**
Past	essendo stato/a/i/e	avendo avuto	avendo abitato	avendo ripetuto	essendo partito/a/i/e

☞ • The gerund is used to indicate an action that specifies or modifies the principal action:
Andando a scuola, ho visto Enzo. *While I was going to school, I saw Enzo.*
Avendo mangiato troppo, si sentì male. *Having eaten too much, he felt sick.*

• The gerund (particularly the past gerund) is rarely used and is normally replaced by explicit phrases:
Mentre andavo a scuola, ho visto Enzo. *While I was going to school, I saw Enzo.*
Poiché aveva mangiato troppo, si sentì male. *As he had eaten too much, he felt sick.*

• The past gerund is formed from the present gerund of the auxiliary **avere** or **essere** and the past participle of the verb.

• The present gerund is also used to indicate progressive action: **stare + gerund**:
Sto studiando il gerundio. *I am studying the gerund.*
Stavo partendo per l'Italia. *I was leaving for Italy.*

Present	ESSERE	AVERE	ABITARE	RIPETERE	PARTIRE
Perfect	essere stato/a/i/e	aver avuto	aver abitato	aver ripetuto	essere partito/a/i/e

☞   The infinitive usually depends on another verb or is used in secondary clauses:
Devo **scrivere** a Giovanna. *I have to write to Giovanna.*
Non è più andato in quel ristorante dopo **essere stato** male.
He didn't go to that restaurant any more after being ill.

☞   The infinitive can be used:
- to give an order:
Rallentare. *Slow down.* Dare la precedenza *Give way.*
- to form the imperative with **tu**:
Non urlare! *Don't shout!*
- to give instruction:
Scrivere in stampatello. *Write in block letters.*
- as a noun:
Nuotare è rilassante. *Swimming is relaxing.* Ballare è divertente. *Dancing is enjoyable.*

☞   The present infinitive can be used to indicate an action in preparation: **stare + per + infinitive**:
Sto per uscire. *I'm about to go out.* Stavo per partire. *I was going to leave.*

Preposition and the infinitive

☞   Some verbs are followed by the infinitive without a preposition. Among these verbs are:
potere (to be able), **dovere** (to have to), **volere** (to want):
Posso chiederti un favore? *Can I ask you a favour?*
Devo studiare. *I have to study.* Vorrei andare al cinema. *I'd like to go to the cinema.*

☞   **Common verbs with a preposition before the infinitive are:**

cominciare a	*to start*
continuare a	*to go on*
imparare a	*to learn*
insegnare a	*to teach*
decidere di	*to decide*
dimenticare di	*to forget*
cercare di	*to try*
promettere di	*to promise*
smettere di	*to stop*
sperare di	*to hope*

e.g.   Ha cominciato a lavorare. *He started working.*
Ho dimenticato di spedire la cartolina. *I forgot to send the card.*

7.15 Reflexive Verbs (Verbi Riflessivi)

INDICATIVE

	PRESENT (I enjoy myself, ...)	PERFECT (I have enjoyed myself, ...)	
(Io)	**mi** diverto	mi sono divertito/a	myself
(tu)	**ti** diverti	ti sei divertito/a	yourself (informal)
(lui, lei ,Lei)	**si** diverte	si è divertito/a	himself, herself, yourself (formal)
(noi)	**ci** divertiamo	ci siamo divertiti/e	ourselves
(voi)	**vi** divertite	vi siete divertiti/e	yourselves
(loro)	**si** divertono	si sono divertiti/e	themselves

e.g. Mi lavo. *I wash myself.*
Ci siamo lavati. *We have washed ourselves.*
Si è bruciata. *She has burnt herself.*

Note

☞ *The reflexive form is generally used when the subject of the verb is the same as the object.*
☞ *The pronouns **mi, ti, si, ci, vi** precede the verb.*
☞ *They follow the verb, joining with it in a single word, only in the following cases:*
  • *with the imperative (**tu, noi**): Vestiti! (Get dressed!) Vestiamoci! (Let's get dressed!)*
  • *with the past participle: Vestitosi, è uscito. (After getting dressed, he went out.)*
  • *with the infinitive: Bisogna vestirsi. (We must get dressed.)*
  • *with the gerund: Ha perso un bottone vestendosi. (He lost a button while getting dressed.)*
☞ *In compound tenses the auxiliary **essere** is always used.*

The most common reflexive verbs are:

ABBRONZARSI	*to get tanned*	INTERESSARSI A/DI	*to take an interest in*
ABITUARSI A	*to accustom oneself*	LAMENTARSI	*to complain*
ACCOMODARSI	*to come in; to sit down*	PERDERSI	*to get lost*
ALZARSI	*to get up; to stand up*	PETTINARSI	*to comb one's hair*
ANNOIARSI	*to be bored*	PREPARARSI	*to get ready*
ARRABBIARSI	*to get angry*	PREOCCUPARSI	*to worry*
AVVICINARSI A	*to approach*	ROMPERSI	*to break*
BRUCIARSI	*to burn oneself*	SBRIGARSI	*to be quick, to hurry up*
CHIAMARSI	*to be called*	SCUSARSI	*to apologize*
CONGRATULARSI CON	*to congratulate*	SENTIRSI	*to feel*
DIVERTIRSI	*to enjoy oneself*	SVEGLIARSI	*to wake up*
FERMARSI	*to stop*	VERGOGNARSI	*to be ashamed*
INCONTRARSI	*to meet*	VESTIRSI	*to get dressed*

8. NUMERALS (NUMERALI)

CARDINALS (1, 2, ...)	ORDINALS (first, second, ...)
1 uno,-a	primo, -a, -i, -e
2 due	secondo, ...
3 tre	terzo
4 quattro	quarto
5 cinque	quinto
6 sei	sesto
7 sette	settimo
8 otto	ottavo
9 nove	nono
10 dieci	decimo
11 undici	undicesimo
12 dodici	dodicesimo
13 tredici	tredicesimo
14 quattordici	quattordicesimo
15 quindici	quindicesimo
16 sedici	sedicesimo
17 diciassette	diciassettesimo
18 diciotto	diciottesimo
19 diciannove	diciannovesimo
20 venti	ventesimo
21 ventuno	ventunesimo
22 ventidue	ventiduesimo
23 ventitré	ventitreesimo
28 ventotto	ventottesimo
30 trenta	trentesimo
40 quaranta	quarantesimo
50 cinquanta	cinquantesimo
60 sessanta	sessantesimo
70 settanta	settantesimo
80 ottanta	ottantesimo
90 novanta	novantesimo
100 cento	centesimo
101 centouno	centunesimo
200 duecento	duecentesimo
400 quattrocento	quattrocentesimo
500 cinquecento	cinquecentesimo
900 novecento	novecentesimo
1.000 mille	millesimo

1.001 milleuno	1976 millenovecentosettantasei
1.002 milledue	1977 millenovecentosettantasette
1.003 milletré	1978 millenovecentosettantotto
1800 milleottocento	1990 millenovecentonovanta
1975 millenovecentosettantacinque	1991 millenovecentonovantuno

2.000 duemila
10.000 diecimila
100.000 centomila
1.000.000 un milione

Continued ➡

8.1 Cardinal Numbers

☞ Gender and plural.
- **Zero** takes the plural: due zeri, tre zeri, ...
- **Uno** takes the feminine and follows the rules of the indefinite article: uno studente, una studentessa, ...
- The plural of **mille** is **-mila** (1.000 = mille ; 2.000 = duemila; 400.000 = quattrocentomila).
- **Milione, bilione, miliardo,** etc. take the plural (milioni, bilioni, miliardi, etc.) and link to the noun that follows them by means of the preposition **di**: due milioni di abitanti, tre miliardi di lire, ...
- All other numbers are invariable: due studenti, due studentesse, ...

☞ **Tre** has an accent in compound numbers: ventitré, centotré, ...

☞ There is elision when **uno** and **otto** follow **venti, trenta, quaranta** , etc.: ventuno, trentotto, trentuno, trentotto, ...

☞ When **cento** and **mille** are followed by another number, they can also be written separated by **e**: 101 = cento e uno; 1.080 = mille e ottanta, ...

☞ In Italian a full stop is used when a comma is used in English and viceversa: 1.000=*1,000*

☞ Colloquially abbreviations are often used, particularly to indicate the hundreds above a thousand: tremila e due = tremila e duecento. Novemila e cinque = novemila e cinquecento.

☞ Arabic numerals are used in general:
- to avoid excessively long words: 24.546 lire (but in cheques, current accounts, etc. they are also written in one word: ventiquattromilacinquecentoquarantasei lire.)
- in dates: 2 maggio, 6 giugno, ... (with the exception of the first day of the month: 1° maggio, 1° giugno, ...)

☞ Common idiomatic phrases: in due parole (in a few words); è qui a due passi (is only just around the corner).

8.2 Ordinal Numbers

☞
- Ordinal numbers are variable: primo, prima, primi, prime, ...
- Apart from the first ten, they are formed by adding **-esimo** to the cardinal numbers without the last vowel: undicesimo, dodicesimo, ...
- They can be written in two ways: I, II, ... or 1°, 1ᵃ , 2°, 2ᵃ , ...

8.3 Fractions

☞
- 1/2 (un mezzo or una metà), 1/3 (un terzo), 1/4 (un quarto), 1/5 (un quinto), 1/6 (un sesto), 2/2 (due mezzi), 2/3 (due terzi), 3/4 (tre quarti), ...
- **Mezzo** agrees with the noun to which it refers (e.g .mezzo litro di vino, mezza bottiglia), but usually when it follows the noun it is invariable (e.g. è l'una e mezzo, sono le due e mezzo).

8.4 Multiple Numbers
- **Doppio** (double), **triplo** (triple), **quadruplo** (quadruple), **quintuplo** (quintuple), etc.

8.5 Collective Numbers
- **Paio** (pair; a couple), **coppia** (couple; pair), **decina** (ten; about ten), **dozzina** (dozen; about a dozen), ... **centinaio** (a hundred; about a hundred), **migliaio** (thousand; about a thousand) Plural: paia, coppie, decine, dozzine, ... centinaia, migliaia.
- **Entrambi** (both) takes the feminine: entrambi i ragazzi, entrambe le ragazze. **Ambedue** (both) is invariable: ambedue i ragazzi, ambedue le ragazze.

8.6 Iterative Numbers
- Una volta (once), due volte (twice), tre volte (three times), etc.

8.7 Mathematical Signs
- + (più), - (meno), x (**moltiplicato** per), : (**diviso** per), = (uguale a), % (per cento).

9. DATES AND TIME (LA DATA E L'ORA)

9.1 Calendar

Che data è oggi?	*What is the date today?*	È il due di novembre.	*It is the second of November.*
Quanti ne abbiamo?	*What day is it today?*	Ne abbiamo tre.	*It is the third.*
Che giorno è oggi?	*Which day of the week is it today?*	È lunedì.	*It is Monday.*

Giorni (Days):   lunedì, martedì, mercoledì, giovedì, venerdì, sabato, domenica.
Monday, Tuesday, Wednesday, Thursday, Friday, Saturday, Sunday.

Mesi (Months):
gennaio, febbraio, marzo, aprile, maggio, giugno, luglio, agosto, settembre, ottobre,novembre, dicembre.
January, February, March, April, May, June, July, August, September, October, November, December.

Stagioni (Seasons):   primavera, estate, autunno, inverno.
spring, summer, autumn, winter.

Note

☞ • *The ordinal number is used only for the first day of the month: è il primo (di) novembre.*
• *The names of the months and of the days of the week are nearly
always written with a small letter.*

9.2 Clock

a che ora?	*at what time?*	ora	*hour*
alle nove	*at nine o'clock*	precise (alle due ...)	*at two o'clock sharp*
avanti di tre minuti	*three minutes fast*	preciso	*exact, precise*
che ora è/che ore sono?	*what time is it?*	quando?	*when?*
è l'una	*it is one o'clock*	quarto	*quarter*
indietro di sei minuti	*six minutes slow*	secondo	*second*
mezz'ora	*half an hour*	sono le due e cinque	*it's five past two*
mezzanotte	*midnight*	sono le due meno cinque	*it's five to two*
mezzo/mezza	*half*	sono le tre e mezzo	*it's half past three*
mezzogiorno	*midday*	sono le tre e un quarto	*it's a quarter past three*
minuto	*minute*	sono le tre	*it's three o'clock*

☞ • To tell the time in colloquial Italian only the cardinal numbers from 1 to 12 are normally
used: Faccio colazione alle sette e venti (7.20). Di solito ceniamo alle sette e venti (19.20).
I have breakfast at seven twenty . We usually have supper at seven twenty.
• The cardinal numbers from 1 to 24 are used for timetables of trains, airlines, etc.
Il treno per Pisa parte alle venti e trenta (20.30). *The train to Pisa leaves at twenty thirty (20:30).*

9.3 Expressions of Time with 'Da' and 'Per'

da (for)	Abito a Londra **da** sei anni. (I've been living in London for six years.)
	Studio italiano **da** due anni. (I've been studying Italian for two years.)
da (since)	Non li vediamo **dalle** sette. (We haven't seen them since seven o'clock.)
da (as from,from)	**Da** oggi in poi. (From today onwards.)
per (for)	Ho studiato italiano **per** due anni. (I studied Italian for two years.)
per (by)	Sarà pronto **per** lunedì. (It will be ready by Monday.)

10. PREPOSITIONS (PREPOSIZIONI SEMPLICI)

The most used prepositions are:

> **di, a, da, in, con, su, per, tra/fra**

DI (of, by, from)
- Vorrei una scatola **di** cioccolatini. *I'd like a box of chocolates.*
- È un film **di** Fellini. *It's a film by Fellini.*
- **Di** dove sei? *Where are you from?*

A (to, at, in)
- Vado **a** Londra. *I'm going to London.*
- Resto **a** casa. *I'm staying at home.*
- Abito **a** Padova. *I live in Padua.*

DA (from, to, by, at)
- **Da** dove vieni? *Where do you come from?*
- Andiamo **da** Bruno? *Shall we go to Bruno's?*
- Sono conosciuti **da** tutti. *They are known by everyone.*
- Siamo stati tutta la mattina **da** Giovanna. *We've been at Giovanna's all morning.*

IN (in, to, at, by)
- È **in** giardino. *He's in the garden.*
- Vado **in** Australia. *I'm going to Australia.*
- Non è **in** casa. *He's not at home.*
- Verremo **in** treno. *We'll come by train.*

PER (for, through, to)
- Ho un regalo per te. *I have a present for you.*
- È passato per i campi. *He went through the fields.*
- Vorrei un biglietto **per** Pisa. *I'd like a ticket to Pisa.*

CON (with)
- È uscita **con** Elena. *She's gone out with Elena.*

SU (on)
- La borsa è **su** quella poltrona. *The bag is on that chair.*

TRA/ FRA (between, among, in)
- Arriverà tra l'una e le due. *He'll arrive between one and two.*
- **Tra** gli invitati, ci sono quattro americani. *There are four Americans among the guests.*
- Torno **fra** dieci minuti. *I'll be back in ten minutes.*

Note

- *These prepositions have no meaning of their own and therefore cannot be translated literally; the translation given refers to the most common use.*
- *Di can take an apostrophe in front of a vowel: d'inverno, d'origine.*
- *Da takes an apostrophe only in front of a few expressions: d'altra parte, d'altronde, d'ora in poi.*
- *A can take d in front of a vowel for phonetical reasons: andiamo ad Alassio, ad esempio.*
- *Tra=Fra the choice only depends on phonetics: tra i fratelli, fra le traduzioni.*

	+ il	lo	la	l'	i	gli	le
a	al	allo	alla	all'	ai	agli	alle
da	dal	dallo	dalla	dall'	dai	dagli	dalle
su	sul	sullo	sulla	sull'	sui	sugli	sulle
di	del	dello	della	dell'	dei	degli	delle
in	nel	nello	nella	nell'	nei	negli	nelle

e.g.   Partirò **alle** sei. *I'll leave at six.*
Vada dritto fino **all'**incrocio. *Go straight on as far as the crossing.*
È andata **dalla** sua amica. *She's gone to her friend's.*
Bisogna salire **sul** terrazzo, *It's necessary to go up to the terrace.*
La camicia è nel cassetto. *The shirt is in the drawer.*
Verrà **con le** sue cugine, *She'll come with her cousins.*
Grazie **per l'**ospitalità! *Thank you for the hospitality!*

- *With the prepositions **con** and **per** the union with the article is optional but is now considered obsolete and in some cases can cause ambiguity of meaning (**collo, colla, pelle** also mean neck, glue, skin/leather).*
- ***Tra** and **fra** are never joined to the article: L'ho trovato **tra i** miei vestiti.*

11. CONJUNCTIONS (CONGIUNZIONI)

COMMON CONJUNCTIONS

Conjunctions joining two words in a single phrase or two separate phrases

E (and)	Ha i capelli corti **e** lisci. *Her hair is short and straight.*
(**ed** in front of a vowel)	Ha salutato tutti **ed** è uscito. *He said goodbye to everybody and went out.*
Anche (also; too)	C'erano **anche** i suoi genitori. *His parents were there too.*
O (or)	Arriveranno oggi **o** domani. *They will arrive today or tomorrow.*
Ma, **però** (but; however)	Lei è simpatica, **ma** suo fratello è troppo arrogante.
	She is nice, but her brother is too arrogant.
	Non potrò andare alla sua festa, **però** gli ho spedito un regalo.
	I won't be able to go to his party, however I sent him a present.
Infatti (in fact)	Sono già partiti, **infatti** le persiane sono chiuse.
	They've already left, in fact the shutters are closed.
Dunque, perciò	L'autobus è appena passato, **perciò** dovremo andare a piedi.
(so; therefore)	*The bus has just gone, so we'll have to walk.*
	Dunque faremo così! *Therefore we'll do this!*
Sia...sia	Abbiamo invitato **sia** i tuoi amici **sia** quelli di tuo fratello.
(both ... and; whether ... or)	*We've invited both your friends and your brother's.*
O... o (either ... or)	Sono andati **o** a ballare **o** al cinema.
	They've either gone dancing or to the cinema.
Non solo ... ma anche	È un film **non solo** noioso **ma anche** lungo.
(not only ... but also)	*It's a film that's not only boring but also long.*
Né ... né	Non vuole **né** pane **né** grissini.
(neither...nor)	*He doesn't want either bread or bread sticks.*
(either...or)	

Conjunctions joining two or more phrases, of which one is governed by the other

Che (that)	Spero **che** tu stia meglio. *I hope you are better.*
Se (if)	Non sappiamo **se** inviterà Giorgio. *We don't know if she'll invite Giorgio.*
Perché (because)	Non sono venuto **perché** non stavo bene.
	I didn't come because I wasn't well.
Poiché (as, since)	**Poiché** piove, restiamo a casa. *As it's raining, we'll stay at home.*
Come se (as if).	Fai **come se fossi** a casa tua. *Behave as if you were at home.*
Anche se (even if)	**Anche** se lavorassi tutta la notte, non riuscirei a finire.
	Even if I worked all night, I wouldn't manage to finish.
Se (if; whether; unless)	**Se** ci sarà il sole, andremo al mare.
	If the sun is out, we'll go to the seaside.
A condizione che	Andranno al mare, **a condizione** che non piova.
(provided that)	*They'll go to the seaside provided that it's not raining.*
Quando (when)	Uscirai **quando** avrai finito i compiti!
	You'll go out when you've finished your homework!
Mentre (while)	**Mentre** andavo a scuola, ho incontrato Claudio.
	I met Claudio while I was going to school.

An accent is added:

- on words of two or more syllables when the stress falls on the vowel of the last syllable.
  e.g. Qualità, laggiù, università, perché, però, partì, andò, andrà, ventitré, lunedì, etc.

- on the following monosyllables: **può, già, più, ciò** and **giù.**

- on some monosyllables to distinguish them from other words with the same form
  but different meanings:

è verb (he/she/it is)	**e** conjunction (and)
dà verb (he/she/it gives)	**da** preposition (from,to, ...)
là adverb of place (there)	**la** article, pronoun (the; her)
lì adverb of place (there)	**li** pronoun (them)
né conjunction (nor, ...)	**ne** pronoun and adverb (of this, from here, ...)
sì affirmative (yes)	**si** pronoun, impersonal, passive (himself, one, ...)
sé pronoun (himself, ...)	**se** conjunction (if, whether)
tè noun (tea)	**te** pronoun (you)

e.g.   Lui **è** italiano **e** loro sono inglesi. *He is Italian and they are English.*
Lui **dà** il libro a Pietro. Viene **da** Firenze. *He gives the book to Pietro. He comes from Florence.*
La penna è **là** sul tavolo. **La** vedi? *The pen is there on the table. Can you see it?*
I libri sono **lì** accanto alla penna. **Li** vedi? *The books are there close to the pen. Can you see them?*
Né lui **né** lei. **Ne vuoi** ancora? *Neither him nor her. Would you like some more of it?*
Pensa solo a **sé**. **Se** finirò i compiti, andrò al cinema. *He thinks only about himself. If I finish my homework, I will go to the cinema.*
Sì, sono americano. **Si** dice che sia americano. *Yes, I am American. He is said to be American.*
Hai comperato il **tè**? Beato **te**! *Did you buy the tea? Lucky you!*

- The others monosyllables are not accented.
  e.g. Va, fa, su, sto, sta, qui, qua, tra, fra, me, so, fu, no, etc.

Note

☞   *The Italian accents on the last vowel are :*
- *acute on closed é : né, sé, perché, poiché, ripeté, ventitré.*
- *grave on open è and , usually, on the other vowels (à, ù, ò and ì):*
  è, caffè, però, perciò, tè, già, più, così, etc.
- *The difference between the two types of accents is diminishing and it is common to add a grave accent to all vowels when necessary.*

☞   - *Sé may be reinforced by the word stesso and in this case is usually not accented. The use of an accent is nevertheless common and acceptable, particularly in places where the meaning may be ambiguous (sé stessi, sé stesse, without an accent could also mean "if I were, if she/he were")*

☞   - *Remember that:*
  - the preposition a and the verb ha are never accented:
  - a silent h is added to distinguish ho (I have), ha (he/she/it has), hai (you have), hanno (they have), from o (or), a (to), ai (to the), and anno (year).

13. LANGUAGE FUNCTIONS (WHAT WE DO WITH THE LANGUAGE)

13.1 Greeting People

Ciao!
Salve!
Buongiorno!
Buongiorno, signor/signora/signorina...
Buonasera...

Hallo!, Hi.
Hallo!
Good morning!/Good afternoon!
Good morning, Mr./Mrs/Miss
Good evening ...

13.2 Introducing Someone And Being Introduced

Questo/questa è ...
Le presento il signor...[formal]
Posso presentarle il signor... [formal]

Mi chiamo...
Ciao, (io sono Carla).
Piacere!
Molto lieto! [formal]

This is ...
This is Mr...
May I introduce Mr... to you?

My name is ...
Hallo! (I am Carla).
How do you do?
How do you do?

13.3 Taking Leave

Ciao!
(Ciao), a presto!
Arrivederci!
ArrivederLa! [formal]
Buonanotte!
A più tardi!
A domani!

Bye!
See you soon!
Goodbye!
Goodbye!
Good night!
See you later!
See you tomorrow!

13.4 Attracting Attention

Scusa...
(Mi) scusi... [formal]
Senta, per favore... [formal]

Excuse me....
Excuse me...
Excuse me, please...

13.5 Congratulating

Bravo!
Congratulazioni!
Sei stato bravissimo!

Well done!
Congratulations!
You've done very well!

13.6 Expressing Good Wishes

Auguri!
I migliori auguri!
Ti auguro...
Le auguro...[formal]
Buon Natale!
Buon Anno!
Buona Pasqua!
Buon compleanno!
Buone vacanze!
Buon viaggio!

Best wishes!
All the best!
I wish you..
I wish you..
Merry Christmas!
Happy New Year!
Happy Easter!
Happy Birthday!
Have a good holiday!
Have a good trip!

13.7 Expressing And Responding To Thanks

Grazie!
Grazie mille!
Grazie per ...
Ti ringrazio!
La ringrazio. [formal]
Non so come ringraziarti!
Non so come ringraziarLa! [formal]
Prego!
Di niente!
È stato un piacere!

Thanks!
Thanks a lot/ thank you very much!
Thank you for ...
Thank you!
Thank you!
I don't know how to thank you!
I don't know how to thank you!
Don't mention it!
It's all right!
It has been a pleasure!

13.8 Expressing Lack Of Understanding

Come, (scusa)?
Scusi, come ha detto? [formal]
Prego? (Non ho capito!)
Non capisco.
Non ho capito.

Vuole ripetere, prego? [formal]
Che cosa vuol dire?
Puoi ripetere, per favore?
Non è chiaro.
E cioè?

Pardon?
(I beg your) pardon?
(I beg your) pardon?
I don't understand.
I haven't understood.

Would you repeat it, please?
What does it mean?
Can you repeat it, please?
It is not clear.
What do you mean?

13.9 Expressing Agreement And Disagreement

Sono d'accordo.
Hai (proprio) ragione!
Naturalmente!
Giusto!

Non sono d'accordo!
Sbagli!
Non è vero!
Per niente!

I agree.
You're right!
Of course!
Right!

I don't agree!
You are wrong!
It's not true!
Not at all!

Continued

13.10 Expressing Surprise

Che sorpresa!
Che bella sorpresa!
Questa sì che è una sorpresa!
Davvero!
Non ci credo!
No!

What a surprise!
What a nice surprise!
This is a real surprise!
No kidding?
I can't believe it!
No!

13.11 Expressing Hope

Speriamo!
Speriamo di sì.
Magari!
Speriamo che tu stia meglio!
[see 7.11 Subjunctive]

Let's hope so!
I hope so!
If only!
I hope you'll be better.

13.12 Expressing Satisfaction

Magnifico!
Che bello!
Sono contento/soddisfatto ...
È proprio quello che desideravo.
È molto bello!

Wonderful!
How lovely!
I'm very happy/satisfied ...
It's just what I wanted.
It's lovely!

13.13 Expressing Gratitude

Ti sono molto grato ...
Le sono molto grato... [formal]
Sei stato molto gentile...
È stato molto gentile... [formal]
La ringrazio! [formal]
Grazie di tutto!

I am very grateful to you ...
I am very grateful to you ...
You've been very kind...
It was very kind of you...
Thank you!
Thanks for everything!

13.14 Apologizing

Scusa!
Scusi! [formal]
Scusami (tanto)!
Mi scuso per ...
Mi dispiace!

Sorry!
Sorry!
I am so sorry!
I apologize for ...
I am sorry!

13.15 Expressing Indifference

Non mi interessa!
Per me è lo stesso.
Fai come vuoi!

I don't care!
It's all the same to me.
Do as you like!

Continued

13.16 Suggesting A Course Of Action (Including The Speaker)

Andiamo ...?
Potremmo ...
Vieni con noi ...?
Ti andrebbe di ...?
Le andrebbe di ... ? [formal]

Shall we go ...?
We could ...
Will you come with us ...?
Would you like to ...?
Would you like to ...?

13.17 Requesting Others To Do Something

Potresti ...?
Potrebbe ...? [formal]
Ti spiacerebbe ...?
Le spiacerebbe ...? [formal]
Le sarei molto grato se potesse ...

Could you ...?
Could you ...?
Would you mind...?
Would you mind ...?
I would be very grateful if you could ...

13.18 Asking For Advice

Che ne pensi ...?
Hai qualche idea?
Che cosa faresti (al mio posto)?
Che cosa mi consigli?
Che cosa mi consiglia? [formal]

What do you think of ...?
Any ideas?
What would you do (in my situation?)
What do you suggest?
What would you suggest?

13.19 Advising Others (Not) To Do Something

Secondo me, dovresti ...
Ti consiglio ...
Le consiglio ... [formal]
(Non) dovresti ...
Faresti meglio a ...
Perché non ...?

In my opinion, you should...
I suggest that you ...
I suggest that you ...
You should ... (You should not)...
You'd better ...
Why not ...?

13.20 Giving And Seeking Permission To Do Something

Puoi ...
Certamente!
Naturalmente!

Posso ...?
Potrei ...?
Ti dispiace se ...?
Le dispiace se ... ? [formal]

You can ...
Certainly!
Of course!

May I ...?
Could I ...?
Do you mind if ...?
Do you mind if ...?

Note

For a more detailed description of communicative functions and application in the appropriate context, see **Pronti .... Via! The Italian Handbook.**

14. "FALSE FRIENDS"

English/Italian "false friends" are words that are apparently similar but actually have different meanings.

e.g. LIBRERIA = bookshop; bookcase   LIBRARY = biblioteca

Here follows a list of some common "false friends". If you learn them, you will be able to avoid some of the biggest pitfalls in oral and, more particularly, reading comprehension.

ITALIAN	ENGLISH
ARGOMENTO = subject, topic, point	ARGUMENT = discussione, controversia
ASSUMERE = to take on, to engage	TO ASSUME = supporre, assumere
ATTUALMENTE = at present, at the moment	ACTUALLY = realmente, effettivamente, in effetti, …
CANTINA = cellar	CANTEEN = mensa, portaposate
COLLEGIO = boarding school	COLLEGE = 'college', università, politecnico, …
COMPLESSIONE = constitution	COMPLEXION = carnagione, aspetto
CONFETTI = sugar-coated almonds	CONFETTI = coriandoli
CONFIDENZA = familiarity, intimacy	CONFIDENCE = fiducia, sicurezza (di sé), confidenza
CONVENIENTE = suitable, cheap, advantageous	CONVENIENT = comodo
EDUCAZIONE = (good) manners, upbringing	EDUCATION = istruzione, educazione
EVENTUALMENTE = perhaps, if necessary	EVENTUALLY = alla fine, in conclusione, finalmente
FACILITÀ = ease, facility	FACILITIES = attrezzature
FATTORIA = farm	FACTORY = fabbrica
MAGAZZINO = warehouse, department store	MAGAZINE = rivista, periodico
MORBIDO = soft; delicate	MORBID = morboso
PARENTE = relative	PARENT = genitore
PAVIMENTO = floor	PAVEMENT = marciapiede
PETROLIO = petroleum, crude oil	PETROL = benzina
POSSIBILMENTE = if possible	POSSIBLY = può darsi, forse, …
REGISTRAZIONE = recording	REGISTRATION = iscrizione
RUMORE = noise	RUMOUR = voce, diceria
SENSIBILE = sensitive	SENSIBLE = sensato, ragionevole
SOPPORTARE = to stand, to bear	TO SUPPORT = mantenere, sostenere, tifare.

15. VOCABULARY

(R) = Receptive: is used to indicate words which only need to be understood for reading and listening rather than for active use in conversation. Basic level words followed by (R) should however be used actively at the higher level.

Higher level Italian words appear in bold.

In general nouns ending in -o are masculine, those ending in -a are feminine. Irregular nouns are indicated by (m) when masculine, (f) when feminine. Singular nouns ending in -e can be masculine or feminine and are indicated accordingly by (m) or (f). Other abbreviations used are (pl.) for plural and (sing.) for singular.

VOCABULARY LISTS BY TOPIC

PERSONAL IDENTIFICATION

Name

chi?	who?
chiamarsi	to be called
cognome (m)	surname (R)
compilare	to fill in
essere	to be
firma	signature (R)
firmare	to sign (R)
identità	identity
in stampatello	in block letters (R)
modulo	form (R)
nome (m)	name
riempire	to fill in
ripetere	to repeat
scrivere	to write
signora	Mrs., Madam
signore (m)	Mr., Sir
signorina	Miss, Madam

Home Address

abitare	to live, to dwell
appartamento	flat
ascensore (m)	lift
casa	home, house
codice postale (m)	post code (R)

corso	main street
destra	right
indirizzo	address
numero	number
paese (m)	country, village
palazzo	building, mansion, block of flats
piano	floor, storey (R)
piazza	square
primo	first
provincia	province (R)
regione (f)	region
sinistra	left
via	road, street
viale (m)	avenue

Telephone

dare	to give
fare il numero	to dial
gettone (m)	token
inserire	to insert
mettere	to put
numero	number
prefisso	area code (telephone) (R)
telefonare	to telephone

Age and Birthday

anni	years
anziano	old, elderly
avere	to have
compleanno	birthday
data di nascita	date of birth (R)
essere nato	to have been born
età	age
gennaio, ecc.	January, etc.
già	already
giovane	young
lunedì, ecc.	Monday, etc
luogo di nascita	place of birth (R)
maggiore	older, elder (R)
mese (m)	month
minore	younger (R)
quanti	how many
undicenne, ecc ...	eleven year old, etc ...
vecchio	old

Vocabulary

Nationality and country of residence

America	*America*
americano	*American*
Australia	*Australia*
australiano	*Australian*
bandiera	*flag*
belga	*Belgian*
Belgio	*Belgium*
britannico	*British*
carta di identità	*identity card*
danese	*Danish*
Danimarca	*Denmark*
dove?	*where?*
Europa	*Europe*
europeo	*European*
francese	*French*
Francia	*France*
Galles	*Wales*
gallese	*Welsh*
Germania	*Germany*
Gran Bretagna	*Great Britain*
Grecia	*Greece*
greco	*Greek*
Irlanda	*Ireland*
irlandese	*Irish*
Italia	*Italy*
Italiani	*the Italians*
italiano	*Italian*
lussemburghese	*Luxemburger*
Lussemburgo	*Luxemburg*
nato	*born*
nazione (f)	*nation*
Olanda	*Holland*
olandese	*Dutch*
passaporto	*passport*
Portogallo	*Portugal*
portoghese	*Portuguese*
residenza	*residence (R)*
Russia	*Russia*
russo	*Russian*
Scozia	*Scotland*
scozzese	*Scottish*
Spagna	*Spain*
spagnolo	*Spanish*
straniero	*foreigner*
tedesco	*German*

Occupations

assistente di volo (m/f)	*steward, stewardess*
autista (m/f)	*driver*
avvocato	*lawyer*
bene	*well*
cameriere (m)	*waiter*
casalinga	*housewife*
commerciante (m/f)	*trader*
commercio	*trade*
commesso	*shop-assistant*
dentista (m/f)	*dentist*
direttore (m)	*manager*
disoccupato	*unemployed*
ditta	*firm, company*
diventare	*to become*
dottore (m)	*doctor*
essere	*to be*
fabbrica	*factory (R)*
farmacista (m/f)	*chemist, pharmacist*
fattoria	*farm (R)*
guadagnare	*to earn*
impiegato	*employee*
infermiere (m)	*male nurse*
infermiera	*nurse*
insegnante (m/f)	*teacher*
interessante	*interesting*
lavorare	*to work*
lavoro	*job, work*
macellaio	*butcher*
maestro	*teacher (primary)*
magazzino	*store, warehouse*
male	*badly*
meccanico	*mechanic*
medico	*doctor*
negozio	*shop*
operaio	*workman*
padrone (m)	*owner*
paga	*pay, salary*
parrucchiere (m)	*hairdresser*
pizzeria	*'pizzeria'*
poliziotto	*policeman*
posizione (f)	*position*
professione (f)	*occupation, profession*
professore (m)	*teacher, professor*
proprietario	*owner*
salario	*wage*

49

segretario	*secretary*
stipendio	*salary*
studente (m)	*student*
tassista (m/f)	*taxi-driver*
trovare un impiego	*to find a job*
ufficio	*office*

Likes and Dislikes

amare	*to love, to like*
andare matto per	*to be crazy about* (R)
favorito	*favourite*
migliore	*better*
molto	*much, very*
noioso	*boring*
non posso vedere	*I cannot stand/bear* (R)
odiare	*to hate*
ottimo	*very good, excellent*
peggiore	*worse*
piacere	*to like*
poco	*a little*
preferire	*to prefer*
tanto	*a lot*
volere	*to want*

General descriptions

Sex

bambino	*child*
donna	*woman*
femmina	*female*
figlio	*son*
maschio	*male*
ragazza	*girl*
ragazzo	*boy*
signorina	*young lady*
uomo	*man*

Marital status

celibe (m)	*single* (R)
congratularsi con	*to congratulate*
coniugato	*married* (R)
divorziato	*divorced*
fidanzarsi	*to become engaged*
fidanzato	*fiancé*
marito	*husband*

moglie	*wife*
nubile (f)	*single* (R)
scapolo	*bachelor*
separato	*separated*
sposarsi	*to get married*
sposato	*married*
sposo	*bridegroom*
stato civile	*marital status* (R)
vedovo	*widower*

Physical Appearance

a mio parere	*in my opinion*
alto	*tall*
anziano	*old, elderly*
azzurro	*light blue, azure* (R)
baffi (m, pl.)	*moustache* (R)
barba	*beard*
basso	*short*
bellezza	*beauty*
bello	*beautiful, handsome*
ben vestito	*well dressed*
bianco	*white*
biondo	*fair, blonde*
bocca	*mouth*
brutto	*ugly*
capelli (m, pl.)	*hair*
carino	*pretty*
carnagione (f)	*complexion*
castano	*brown, hazel*
chiaro	*fair*
corto	*short*
denti	*teeth*
elegante	*elegant; smart*
giovane	*young*
grasso	*fat*
grazioso	*pretty*
grosso	*big*
lisci (capelli ...)	*straight hair* (R)
lungo	*long*
magro	*thin*
naso	*nose*
nero	*black, dark*
occhi	*eyes*
occhiali	*glasses, spectacles*
ondulato	*wavy* (R)
orecchino	*earring*
orecchio	*ear*

Vocabulary

ricci (capelli ...)	*curly hair (R)*
robusto	*robust, sturdy*
snello	*slim*
somiglianza	*likeness*
sorriso	*smile*
sportivo	*sporty, casual (wear) (R)*
statura media	*average height*
vecchio	*old*
verde	*green (R)*

Character and Disposition

abbastanza	*rather, enough, quite*
allegro	*cheerful, merry*
antipatico	*unpleasant, disagreeable*
beneducato	*well mannered*
bravo	*good, clever*
buffo	*funny*
calmo	*calm*
comprensivo	*understanding*
contento	*happy, pleased*
cortese	*polite*
divertente	*amusing*
felice	*happy*
geloso	*jealous*
gentile	*kind*
intelligente	*intelligent*
maleducato	*bad mannered*
meraviglioso	*wonderful*
molto	*much, very*
nervoso	*irritable, nervous*
noioso	*boring*
onesto	*honest*
orgoglioso	*proud*
pazzo	*crazy*
pigro	*lazy*
piuttosto	*rather*
serio	*serious*
severo	*severe, strict*
simpatico	*nice*
studioso	*studious*
stupido	*stupid*
superbo	*proud, haughty*
timido	*shy, timid*
triste	*sad*
vivace	*vivacious, lively*

FAMILY

Members

amico	*friend*
andare a trovare	*to go and see, to visit*
avere	*to have*
babbo	*dad*
baciare	*to kiss*
bacio	*kiss*
bambino	*child*
cognato	*brother-in-law*
conoscere	*to know*
cugino	*cousin*
famiglia	*family*
figlio	*son*
figlio unico	*only son*
fratello	*brother*
gemelli	*twins*
genitore (m)	*parent*
giovane	*young*
grande	*big, grown-up*
insieme	*together*
madre (f)	*mother*
maggiore	*older*
mamma	*mummy*
marito	*husband*
matrimonio	*marriage, wedding*
minore	*younger*
moglie (f)	*wife*
nipote (m/f)	*nephew, niece, grand-son, grand-daughter*
nonno	*grand-father*
nozze (f, pl.)	*wedding*
numeroso	*numerous; large*
padre (m)	*father*
papà	*daddy*
parente (m/f)	*relative*
piccolo	*small*
presentare	*to introduce*
quanti	*how many*
ragazzo	*boy, boy-friend*
ragazza	*girl, girl-friend*
rassomigliare a	*to look like*
sorella	*sister*
spesso	*often*
suocero	*father-in-law*
unire	*to unite*
zio	*uncle*

Family Pets

abbaiare	*to bark*
accarezzare	*to stroke*
affezionarsi	*to grow fond*
amare	*to love*
ammirare	*to admire*
animale (m)	*animal*
animali domestici	*pets*
avere paura di	*to be afraid of*
bello	*beautiful*
buono	*good*
canarino	*canary*
cane (m)	*dog*
cantare	*to sing*
cavallo	*horse*
criceto	*hamster (R)*
dare da mangiare	*to feed*
docile	*docile*
feroce	*ferocious, fierce*
gabbia	*cage*
gattino	*kitten*
gatto	*cat*
graffiare	*to scratch*
grande	*big*
grosso	*large*
miagolare	*to mew, to miaow (R)*
mordere	*to bite*
pesce (m)	*fish (R)*
piccolo	*small*
preferire	*to prefer*
tartaruga	*tortoise (R)*
temere	*to fear*
uccellino	*little bird*

HOUSE AND HOME

General

abitare	*to live*
affittare	*to let, to rent*
affitto	*rent*
aiuola	*flower-bed*
albero	*tree*
ammobiliato	*furnished (R)*
ampio	*large*
angolo	*corner (R)*
antico	*old, antique*
appartamento	*flat*
ascensore (m)	*lift*
balcone (m)	*balcony*
bello	*beautiful*
ben tenuto	*well kept*
bosco	*wood*
brutto	*ugly*
calmo	*calm, quiet*
caminetto	*fire-place*
campanello	*bell*
cancello	*gate (R)*
caratteristico	*distinctive*
carino	*pretty*
caro	*dear, expensive*
casa	*home, house*
comodità	*comfort*
comodo	*comfortable*
comprare	*to buy*
cortile (m)	*court-yard*
davanti a	*opposite, in front of*
decorare	*to decorate*
dietro	*behind*
difficile	*difficult*
edificio	*building*
entrare	*to enter*
entrata	*entrance*
erba	*grass (R)*
facile	*easy*
fiore (m)	*flower*
garage (m)	*garage*
giardino	*garden*
grande	*big*
in fondo a	*at the end of*
inquilino	*tenant*
isolato	*isolated, remote*

Vocabulary

legno	*wood (R)*	(al piano) di sopra	*upstairs (R)*
località	*area*	(al piano) di sotto	*downstairs (R)*
lontano da	*far from*	al piano superiore	*on the upper floor*
moderno	*modern*	al pianterreno	*on the ground floor*
muro	*wall*	al primo piano	*on the first floor*
nuovo	*new*	aprire	*to open*
padrone di casa (m)	*landlord, owner*	**automobile (f)**	*car*
pagare l'affitto	*to pay the rent*	balcone (m)	*balcony*
palazzo	*building, mansion, block of flats*	**bottone/pulsante (m)**	*button*
		caldo	*hot*
perfetto	*perfect*	camera (da letto)	*bedroom*
piacere	*to like*	**cantina**	*cellar*
piano	*floor, storey*	chiudere	*to shut*
pitturare	*to paint*	confortevole	*comfortable*
plastica	*plastic*	cucina	*kitchen*
portachiave (m)	*key-ring*	dormire	*to sleep*
posate (f, pl.)	*cutlery*	elettricità	*electricity*
prato	*lawn*	elettrico	*electric*
proprio	*own*	entrata	*entrance*
pulito	*clean*	**fiammifero**	*match*
quartiere (m)	*quarter, neighbourhood*	finestra	*window*
quasi	*almost*	**fornello**	*cooker*
roba	*stuff, things*	freddo	*cold*
rumore (m)	*noise*	funzionare	*to work, to function*
rumoroso	*noisy*	gabinetto	*toilet*
solaio	*loft; attic*	garage (m)	*garage*
sopra	*on, over, above*	**ingresso**	*entrance, hallway*
sotto	*under*	**lavandino**	*wash basin, sink*
spazioso	*spacious*	macchina	*car, machine*
specchio	*mirror*	non funziona	*out of order*
sporco	*dirty*	porta	*door*
stanza	*room*	**premere**	*to press (R)*
stretto	*narrow*	**riscaldamento centrale**	*central heating*
suonare	*ring*	**rubinetto**	*tap*
tetto	*roof*	sala da pranzo	*dining room*
trascurato	*neglected (R)*	salotto	*sitting-room, drawing room*
traslocare	*to move (house) (R)*		
veramente	*really*	scale (f, pl.)	*stairs*
vestire	*to dress*	soggiorno	*living-room*
vestirsi	*to get dressed*	**spegnere**	*to switch off*
vicino a	*near*	stanza	*room*
villa	*villa, house*	(stanza da) bagno	*bathroom*
vista	*view*	studio	*study*
		tinello	*(small) dining-room*

Accommodation and Services

accendere	*to switch on*
acqua	*water*

Furniture, household equipment and appliances

apparecchiare	*to lay the table*
armadio	*wardrobe*
arredare	*to furnish*
asciugamano	*hand towel*
aspirapolvere (m)	*vacuum-cleaner*
bagno (vasca da ...)	*bath*
bicchiere (m)	*glass*
bottiglia	*bottle*
caffettiera	*coffee pot*
casseruola	*saucepan*
cassetto	*drawer*
coltello	*knife*
congelatore (m)	*freezer*
coperta	*cover, blanket*
cosa	*thing*
credenza	*sideboard*
cucchiaino	*teaspoon, coffee-spoon*
cucchiaio	*spoon*
cucina	*kitchen*
cuscino	*cushion, pillow*
dentifricio	*toothpaste*
disco	*disc, record*
divano	*settee*
doccia	*shower*
elettricità	*electricity*
elettrico	*electric*
elettrodomestici	*electric household appliances*
federa	*pillow-case*
forchetta	*fork*
forno	*oven*
fotografia	*photograph*
frigorifero	*refrigerator*
giradischi (m)	*record player*
lampada	*lamp*
lampadina	*light bulb*
lavastoviglie (f)	*dish-washer*
lavatrice (f)	*washing machine*
legno	*wood*
lenzuolo	*sheet*
letto	*bed*
libreria	*bookcase (R)*
lucidatrice (f)	*floor-polisher*
mobile (m)	*piece of furniture (R)*
orologio	*clock*
padella	*pan*
paio	*pair*
parecchi	*many, several*
pattumiera	*dustbin*
pentola	*pot; pan (R)*
pianoforte (m)	*piano*
piattino	*saucer*
piatto	*plate, dish*
piumino	*duvet*
poltrona	*arm-chair*
portacenere (m)	*ash-tray*
quadro	*picture*
radio (f)	*radio*
registratore (m)	*tape-recorder*
rotto	*broken*
sapone (m)	*soap*
scaffale (m)	*shelf (R)*
sedia	*chair*
soprammobile (m)	*ornament*
sparecchiare	*to clear the table*
spazzolino da denti	*toothbrush*
sveglia	*alarm clock*
tappeto	*carpet*
tazza	*cup*
tazzina	*coffee-cup*
tegame	*saucepan (R)*
teiera	*tea-pot*
televisione (f)	*television*
tende	*curtains (R)*
tovaglia	*table cloth*
tovagliolo	*napkin, serviette (R)*
video registratore	*video recorder*

Hospitality

accomodarsi	*to sit down*
altrettanto (a te)	*the same to you*
andare a trovare	*to pay a visit*
approfittare	*to take advantage of*
arrivederci	*goodbye*
augurare	*to wish*
aver bisogno di	*to need*
compleanno	*birthday*
contento	*happy*
dire	*to tell, to say*
dovere	*to have to*
entrare	*to enter*
fare visita	*to pay a visit*

Vocabulary

gentile	kind
giornata	day
grazie	thanks
lieto	glad, pleased
molto	much, very
ospitalità	hospitality
partire	to leave
passare	to pass, to spend
per favore/piacere	please
prego!	don't mention it!, you are welcome!
salutare	to greet
sedersi	to sit
si accomodi	take a seat
tanto	much
trascorrere	to spend, to pass
volere	to want, to wish

Life at Home and Daily Routine

abitudine (f)	habit
aiutare	to help
alzarsi	to get up
andare bene	to go well
ascoltare	to listen to
aver bisogno di	to need
badare al bambino	to babysit
cena	supper, evening meal, dinner
ciascuno	every, each, everyone
comprare	to buy
cucinare	to cook
cucire	to sew
di mattina	in the morning
di solito	usually
dormire	to sleep
faccende (f, pl.)	housework
fare colazione	to have breakfast
fare i compiti	to do (one's) homework
fare la spesa	to do the shopping
finalmente	at last
giocare	to play
lavarsi	to wash (oneself)
lavorare	to work
leggere	to read
libro	book
mangiare	to eat
mercato	market
merenda	(afternoon) snack (R)

mettere via	to put away
noia	boredom
ora	hour, now
passatempo	pastime, hobby
pettinarsi	to comb one's hair
pranzo	lunch, main meal
preparare da mangiare	to prepare a meal
pulire	to clean
spolverare	to dust
stirare	to iron
supermercato	supermarket
svegliarsi	to wake up
volentieri	of course, with pleasure, willingly

Spare time job and spending money

abbastanza	enough
avere	to have
bicicletta	bicycle
cominciare	to begin
dare	to give
desiderare	to wish, to want, to like
di buon' ora	early
fare	to make, to do
finire	to finish
giorno	day
guadagnare	to earn
impiegarsi	to be employed, to get a job
lavorare	to work
mancare	to lack
mattina	morning
mese (m)	month
pagare	to pay
permettersi	to take the liberty
pomeriggio	afternoon
quanto	how much
risparmiare	to save
sera	evening
settimana	week
soldi da spendere	spending money
soldi (m, pl.)	money
spendere	to spend
spiccioli (m, pl.)	loose change
sterlina	pound (sterling)
tardi	late
troppo	too much

GEOGRAPHICAL SURROUNDINGS AND WEATHER

Geographical Surroundings

Location

a	*at, to, in*
abitante (m)	*inhabitant*
abitare	*to live*
accanto a	*by, next to, beside*
all'aria aperta	*in the open air*
andare; (... a fare)	*to go; (to ... and do)*
andarsene	*to go away*
avviarsi	*to set off, to be about to*
avvicinarsi a	*to approach*
bordo	*edge*
c'è, ci sono	*there is, there are*
camminare	*to walk*
campagna (in ...)	*country (in the ...)*
capitale (f)	*capital*
centro	*centre*
chilometro	*kilometre*
cielo	*sky*
cima; (in ... a)	*peak; (on the top of)*
circa	*about*
città (in ...)	*city, town (in the ...)*
da	*from, to, by*
davanti a	*in front of; opposite*
destra (a ...)	*right (on the ...)*
di	*of*
dietro (a)	*behind*
dintorni	*surroundings*
dirigersi	*to make for*
distante da	*far from*
distanza	*distance*
distare	*to be, (... a long way from)*
dove, dov'è	*where, where is*
dovunque	*everywhere*
entro	*within, into*
esistere	*to exist, to be*
est (m)	*east*
fare	*to do, to make*
fino a	*as far as*
fondo (in ... a)	*at the end of*
fronte (di ... a)	*in front of*
fuori (di ...)	*outside*
già	*already*

girare	*to go around, to turn*
giro	*tour*
gita	*excursion, trip*
giù	*down*
in	*in, to, at, by*
intorno a	*around*
laggiù	*down there*
lassù	*up there*
là, lì	*there*
località	*locality, place*
lontananza	*distance*
lontano da	*far from*
luogo	*place*
mare; (al ...)	*sea; (at the seaside)*
mezzo (in ... a)	*middle (in the ... of)*
mezzogiorno	*midday*
miglio; (miglia)	*mile; (miles)*
mille	*thousand*
mondo	*world*
montagna (in ...)	*mountain (in the ...s)*
nord (m)	*north*
ovest (m)	*west*
parte; (da questa ...; da nessuna ...)	*side (on this side; nowhere)*
passato	*past*
passeggiare	*to stroll, to walk*
passeggiata	*stroll, walk*
periferia (in ...)	*suburb (in the ...)*
posto	*place*
prendere	*to take*
quaggiù	*down here*
quanto (... ci vuole?)	*how long (... does it take?)*
quanto	*how much*
quassù	*up here*
qui, qua	*here*
regione (f)	*region*
risalire	*to go up again*
ritornare	*to return*
salire	*to go up*
salita	*climb*
scendere	*to descend, to go down*
sinistra (a...)	*left (on the ...)*
sito	*place; situated*
situato	*situated*
situazione (f)	*situation*
sopra	*over, above, on*
sotto	*under, beneath, below*
sperduto	*out of the way (R)*

Vocabulary

● ●

su	*on; over; above*
sud (m)	*south*
terra	*earth, ground, land*
tornare	*to return*
tra/fra	*among; between*
trovarsi	*to find oneself*
vedere	*to see*
venire	*to come*
verso	*towards*
vicino a	*near, next to*
visitare	*to visit*
vista	*view*
vivere	*to live*

Amenities/features of interest

abbastanza	*rather; enough; quite*
aeroporto	*airport*
albergo	*hotel*
albero	*tree*
alto	*high*
altro	*other*
animale (m)	*animal*
annoiarsi	*to be bored*
antico	*ancient*
appena	*just, hardly*
architettura	*architecture*
abbazia	*abbey*
banca	*bank*
basso	*low*
bello	*beautiful*
bene	*well*
bosco	*wood*
brutto	*ugly*
buono	*good*
calmo	*calm*
campeggio	*camping site*
campo	*field, camp*
canale (m)	*canal*
carta geografica	*map*
casa colonica	*farmhouse*
castello	*castle*
cattedrale (f)	*cathedral*
chiasso	*noise (R)*
chiesa	*church*
chiuso	*closed*
cinema (m)	*cinema*
circostante	*surrounding*
colle (m)	*hill, pass*

collina	*hill*
collinoso	*hilly (R)*
coltivare	*to cultivate*
commerciale	*commercial, trade*
concerto	*concert*
conoscere	*to know*
così	*thus*
costa	*coast, shore*
costruito	*built*
credere	*to believe*
discoteca	*discotheque*
divertimento	*amusement*
divertirsi	*to amuse oneself*
dovere	*to have to*
duomo	*cathedral*
edificio	*building*
epoca	*age, epoch*
erba	*grass*
fabbrica	*factory*
fattoria	*farm*
fiore (m)	*flower*
fiume (m)	*river*
fontana	*fountain*
foresta	*forest*
fragore (m)	*noise*
fragoroso	*noisy (R)*
fresco	*fresh*
giardino	*garden*
goder(si)	*to enjoy (oneself)*
grande	*big, large*
grazie a	*thanks to*
importante	*important*
incantevole	*enchanting, delightful*
indicare	*to point out, to show*
industria	*industry*
industriale	*industrial*
insetto	*insect*
interamente	*entirely*
interessante	*interesting*
isola	*island*
lago	*lake*
largo	*wide, large*
lato	*side*
lungo	*long*
lupo	*wolf*
ma	*but*
malgrado	*in spite of*
medievale	*medieval*
meglio	*better, best*

57

● ●

meno	*less*	**presso**	*close to, near (R)*
migliaia	*thousands*	profondo	*deep*
migliore	*better, best*	proprio	*just*
moderno	*modern*	pubblico	*public*
molto	*much, very much*	pulito	*clean*
monotono	*monotonous, dull*	qualche	*some, a few*
monte (m)	*mountain*	quale	*what, which*
monumento	*monument*	quartiere (m)	*district*
municipale	*municipal, local government*	quasi	*almost*
		raro	*unusual, uncommon*
municipio	*town-hall*	**ripido**	*steep*
museo	*museum*	riva	*shore*
negozio	*shop*	riviera	*coast, 'riviera'*
nessuno	*no-one*	**roccia**	*rock*
niente	*nothing*	**roccioso**	*rocky (R)*
noioso	*boring*	rumore (m)	*noise*
nuovo	*new*	**rumoroso**	*noisy*
ogni	*every*	**rurale**	*rural*
opera	*opera*	sapere	*to know*
orto	*vegetable garden*	**sasso**	*stone*
ospedale (m)	*hospital*	**scampagnata**	*trip to the country*
osservare	*to observe, to watch*	scuola	*school*
paesaggio	*landscape, scenery*	**secolo**	*century*
palazzo	*building, block of flats; palace*	sembrare	*to seem, to look like*
		sereno	*clear, fine*
panorama (m)	*view, panorama*	**settentrionale**	*northern*
parco	*park*	**siepe (f)**	*hedge*
parecchio	*quite a lot of*	**sommità**	*top*
parere	*to seem*	spettacolo	*show, sight*
pendio	*slope*	spiaggia	*beach*
però	*however*	sporco	*dirty*
pesca	*fishing*	sport (m)	*sport*
pesce (m)	*fish*	sportivo	*sporting*
piacere	*to like*	stadio	*stadium*
(mi piace, mi piacciono)	*(I like it, I like them)*	stazione (f)	*station*
		stesso	*same*
piacevole	*pleasant*	**stile (m)**	*style*
pianta	*plant*	**storico**	*historic*
picco	*peak*	strada	*street, road*
piccolo	*small*	**stretto**	*narrow*
pietra	*stone*	**stupendo**	*stupendous, marvellous*
piscina	*swimming pool*	**suono**	*sound*
pittoresco	*picturesque*	tanto	*so much, a lot of*
più	*more*	teatro	*theatre*
poco, (pochi)	*little, (few)*	**terreno**	*ground, soil*
podere (m)	*farm*	tranquillo	*quiet, calm*
ponte (m)	*bridge*	**tuttavia**	*nevertheless, yet*
porto	*port*	tutto	*all, everything*
prato	*meadow, lawn*	**uccello**	*bird*

Vocabulary

• •

valle (f)	*valley*
vecchio	*old*
veduta/vista	*view, sight*
viale (m)	*avenue*
villaggio	*village*

Weather

afoso	*sultry*
alba	*dawn*
anno	*year*
asciutto	*dry (R)*
atmosfera	*atmosphere*
autunno	*autumn*
aver caldo/freddo ecc. *to be hot, cold etc.*	
bagnato; (... fradicio) *wet; (soaked) (R)*	
bianco	*white*
bollettino; (... meteorologico) *bulletin;*	
	(weather forecast)
brezza	*breeze*
buio	*dark*
cadere	*to fall*
caldo	*hot*
cambiamento	*change*
cambiare	*to change*
caso	*chance, case*
catinelle (piove a ...) *it rains cats and*	
	dogs (R)
che tempo fa?	*what's the weather like?*
chiaro	*clear*
cielo	*sky*
clima (m)	*climate*
cominciare; (... a fare) *to begin; (... to)*	
coperto	*cloudy, overcast*
correre	*to run*
domani	*tomorrow*
dopodomani	*the day after tomorrow*
estate (f)	*summer*
far bel tempo/bello *to be good weather/fine*	
brutto tempo	*to be bad weather*
caldo	*to be hot*
freddo	*to be cold*
fresco	*cool*
fresco	*fresh*
fulmine (m)	*lightning*
fuori	*outside*
gelare	*to freeze*
generale (in ...)	*in general*

generalmente	*generally*
ghiaccio	*ice*
giorno/giornata	*day*
gradi (centigradi)	*degrees (centigrade)*
grandine (f)	*hail*
ieri	*yesterday*
impermeabile (m)	*raincoat*
indossare	*to put on*
inverno	*winter*
l'altro ieri	*the day before yesterday*
lampeggiare	*to lighten (R)*
lampo	*flash of lightning*
limpido	*clear, limpid (R)*
luce (f)	*light*
luna	*moon*
magnifico	*magnificent, splendid*
mattina/mattinata	*morning*
mese (m)	*month*
metter(si)	*to change*
miglioramento	*improvement*
migliorare	*to improve*
mite	*mild (R)*
nebbia	*fog*
nero	*black*
neve (f)	*snow*
nevicare	*to snow*
nevoso	*snowy (R)*
notte (f)	*night*
nuvola	*cloud*
occhiali, (... da sole) *spectacles, (sun-glasses)*	
oggi	*today*
ogni	*every*
ombra	*shadow, shade*
passato	*past*
peggiorare	*to deteriorate*
pioggia	*rain*
piovere	*to rain*
piovigginare	*to drizzle (R)*
piovoso	*rainy (R)*
poco (fra ...)	*in a short while*
pomeriggio	*afternoon*
precipitazione (f)	*precipitation (R)*
presto	*soon*
prevedere	*to forecast*
previsioni del tempo *weather forecast*	
previsioni meteorologiche *weather*	
	forecast

primavera	spring
prossimo	next
quindicina; (... di giorni)	about fifteen; (a fortnight)
rado (di ...)	seldom
raramente	rarely
ripararsi	to shelter
riparo	shelter
rovescio	downpour
scintillare	to sparkle
scivolare	to slip
scorso	last, past
scroscio	downpour
scuro	dark
sdraiarsi	to lie down
secco	dry
sedia a sdraio	deck-chair
segnare	to indicate
sempre	always
senza	without
sera/serata	evening
sereno	clear, cloudless
settimana	week
sole (m)	sun
soleggiato	sunny
solito; (di ...)	usual; (usually)
splendido	splendid
stagione (f)	season
stella	star
stufo	fed up
sudare	to sweat
sudore (m)	sweat
tempaccio	nasty weather (R)
temperatura	temperature
tempesta	storm
tempestoso	stormy
tempo	time, weather
temporale (m)	thunder storm
termometro	thermometer
tirare	to blow
tramonto	sunset
troppo	too much
tuonare	to thunder
umidità	dampness; humidity
umido	damp
variabile	variable
variazione	variation
vento	wind

visibilità	visibility
zero; (sopra/sotto...)	zero; (above/below...)

TRAVEL AND TRANSPORT

General

affrettarsi	to hurry
andare	to go
a piedi	on foot
arrivare	to arrive
autobus (m)	bus
automobile (f)	car
autostop; (fare l'...)	hitch-hiking; (to hitch-hike)
bicicletta	bicycle
casa	house
comodo	comfortable
di buon' ora	early
diretto	direct
entrare	to enter
fretta (aver ...)	hurry (to be in a ...)
lavoro	work
macchina	machine, car
metropolitana	underground railway
mezzo	means
momento	moment
moneta	coin
motoscafo	motor boat
officina	workshop
partire	to leave
pratico	practical
preferire	to prefer
presto	soon
rapidamente	rapidly; quickly
restare	to stay
rimanere	to stay
ritardo; (in ...)	delay; (late)
ritornare	to return
salire	to get on, to go up
scendere	to get off, to go down
scuola	school
sempre	always
solito; (di ...)	usual; (usually)
spesso	often
spiccioli (m, pl.)	loose change
stesso	same

Vocabulary

● ●

tardi	*late*
tornare	*to return*
trasporto	*transport*
ufficio	*office*
uscire	*to go out*
viaggiare	*to travel*
viaggio	*journey*

Finding the way

accanto a	*next to, near*
aiutare	*to help*
allora	*then*
altrove	*elsewhere*
angolo; (... della strada)	*corner; street corner*
appena	*hardly, as soon as*
attraversare	*to cross,*
avanti	*in front of, ahead*
breve	*brief, short*
c'è, ci sono	*there is, there are*
caffè (m)	*cafè*
camminare	*to walk*
capire	*to understand*
castello	*castle*
centro	*centre*
chiesa	*church*
chilometro	*kilometre*
città	*city, town*
come	*how*
commissariato	*police station*
comunque	*anyhow, however (R)*
continuare	*to continue*
corso	*avenue, main street*
davanti a	*in front of, opposite*
dentro	*inside*
destinazione (f)	*destination*
destra; (a ...)	*right; (on the ...)*
dietro (... a)	*behind*
direzione (f)	*direction*
diritto	*straight*
discoteca	*discotheque*
distanza	*distance*
domandare	*to ask*
dopo	*after*
dove, dov'è?	*where, where is?*
edificio	*building*
ente per il turismo (m)	*tourist board*

entrata	*entry, entrance; admission*
entro	*within*
essere	*to be*
est (m)	*east*
fermata (di autobus)	*bus stop*
fine (f)	*end*
fino a	*as far as*
fondo (in ... a)	*at the bottom of, at the end of*
fronte (di ... a)	*in front of*
garage (m)	*garage*
grazie!	*thank you!*
incontrare	*to meet*
incontro; (andare ... a)	*meeting; (to meet)*
incrocio	*crossing, crossroads*
informare	*to inform*
informazione (f)	*information*
ingresso	*entrance*
laggiù	*down there*
lato	*side*
là	*there*
lontano (da)	*far from*
lungo	*long, along*
marciapiede (m)	*pavement*
mercato	*market*
municipio	*town hall*
museo	*museum*
nessuno	*no-one*
niente; (di ...!)	*nothing; (don't mention it!)*
nord (m)	*north*
ostello della gioventù	*youth hostel*
ovest (m)	*west*
parti; (da queste ...)	*parts; (around here)*
passante (m/f)	*passer-by*
passare	*to pass*
passeggiare	*to stroll, to walk*
passi (a due ... da qui)	*a stone's throw from here*
pedone (m)	*pedestrian*
perdersi	*to get lost*
pianta; (... della città)	*map; (... of the town)*
piazza	*square*
piedi (a ...)	*on foot*
piscina	*swimming pool*
poi	*then*
posto	*place*

potere	to be able	**bar (m)**	bar
prego!	don't mention it!	biglietteria	ticket office
prendere	to take	biglietto (... semplice)	ticket (single ...)
primo, secondo, ecc.	first, second, etc.	biglietto di andata e ritorno	return ticket
proprio	just	binario	platform
qualche	some, a few	bisognare	to need
quale	which	cambiare	to change
questura	police headquarters	camion (m)	lorry
qui	here	**capolinea (m)**	terminus
ringraziare	to thank	**caro**	expensive
ripetere	to repeat	classe (f)	class
ristorante (m)	restaurant	**coda/fila; (fare la ...)**	queue; (to queue up)
salire	to get on, to go up	coincidenza	connection
scendere	to get off, to go down	comprare	to buy
scusi!	excuse me!	**conducente (m/f)**	driver
segnale (m)	signal, sign	**controllore (m)**	inspector (R)
seguire	to follow	corriera	coach
semaforo	traffic lights	costare	to cost
senso, (a ... unico)	direction, (one-way)	**cuccetta**	couchette
servizio	service	**depositare**	to deposit
sindaco	mayor	deposito; (... bagagli)	deposit; (left luggage office)
sinistra; (a ...)	left; (on the...)		
stadio	stadium	diretto a ...	going to ... (R)
stazione (f)	station	domandare	to ask
strada	road, street	facchino	porter
subito	at once	**facoltativo**	optional
sud (m)	south	fare	to make, to do
trattoria	'trattoria', (small) restaurant	fermarsi	to stop
		fermata	stop
trovarsi	to be, to be situated	ferrovia	railway
tutto	all	**filobus (m)**	trolley bus
ufficio postale	post office	**finestrino**	window
uscita	exit	fumare	to smoke
via	road, street	fumatori, (non ...)	smoker, (non-smoker)
vicino a	near, close to, by	gabinetto	toilet
vietato	prohibited	**gente (f, sing.)**	people
volere; (quanto ci vuole per ...?)	to take; (how long does it take to ...?)	**in anticipo**	early
		in piedi	standing
		in ritardo	late
		lento	slow
Public Transport		libero	free
		linea	line
aperto	open	**locomotiva**	locomotive
arrivo; (in ...)	arrival; (arriving)	**mancia**	tip
aspettare	to wait	mezzanotte (f)	midnight
assicurare	to assure, to ensure	mezzogiorno	midday
bagaglio	luggage	nave (f)	ship
banchina	quay	numero	number

Vocabulary

obbligatorio	*obligatory*
occupato	*engaged, occupied*
oggetti smarriti	*lost property*
ora	*time, hour*
orario	*timetable*
pagare	*to pay*
partenza; (in ...)	*departure; (leaving)*
partire	*to leave*
passeggero	*passenger*
perdere	*to lose, to miss*
pericolo	*danger*
pericoloso	*dangerous*
periferia	*suburb*
pianta	*map*
portabagagli	*porter (R)*
portare	*to carry*
portiera	*door*
posto	*place*
prendere	*to take*
prenotare	*to book*
prenotazione (f)	*reservation*
prezzo	*price*
primo	*first*
prossimo	*next*
proveniente da ...	*coming from ... (R)*
pullman (m)	*coach*
quale	*which*
quanto	*how much*
quarto	*quarter*
rapido	*'special express train'*
raramente	*rarely*
ridotto	*reduced*
rischio	*risk*
riservare	*to reserve*
ritardare	*to delay*
sacco	*bag*
sala d'aspetto	*waiting room*
salire	*to get on*
scendere	*to get off*
scompartimento	*compartment*
sedersi	*to sit down*
seduto	*seated*
sobborghi	*suburbs*
soppresso	*cancelled (R)*
sporgersi	*to lean out*
sportello	*door*
stare	*to stay*
stazione (f)	*station*

supplemento	*supplement*
tassì	*taxi*
tram (m)	*tram*
treno, (... locale, diretto, espresso)	*train, (slow, fast, express ...)*
turista (m/f)	*tourist*
ufficio informazioni	*information office*
ultimo	*last*
vagone letto (m)	*sleeping car, sleeper*
valigia	*suitcase*
vettura	*coach, carriage*
viaggiatore (m)	*traveller*
vicino	*near*
vietato	*prohibited*

Travel by Air/Sea

(niente da ...)	*(nothing to ...)*
aereo; (... a reazione)	*aeroplane; (jet)*
aliscafo	*hydrofoil*
aprire	*to open*
assistente di volo (m/f)	*steward, stewardess*
atterrare	*to land (R)*
battello	*boat*
carta d'imbarco	*boarding pass (R)*
chiedere	*to ask*
chiudere	*to close*
cintura di sicurezza	*safety belt (R)*
controllo	*check*
crociera	*cruise*
decollare	*to take off (R)*
dichiarare (qualche cosa da ...)	*declare (something to...)*
dogana	*customs*
doganiere, guardia di finanzia	*customs officer*
frontiera	*frontier*
'hostess'	*air hostess*
hovercraft (m)	*hovercraft (R)*
imbarcare	*to embark, board (R)*
nave (f)	*ship*
passaporto	*passport*
passare	*to pass*
pilota	*pilot*
porto	*port, harbour*
sbarcare	*to disembark (R)*
traghetto (nave ...)	*ferry (boat)*

transatlantico	*(transatlantic) liner*
traversata	*crossing (R)*
uscita	*exit, gate (R)*
volare	*to fly*
volo charter	*charter flight (R)*
volo di linea	*scheduled flight (R)*
volo	*flight*

Private Transport

agente di polizia	*policeman*
allacciare	*to fasten*
andare	*to go*
aria	*air*
arrestare	*to stop*
assicurazione	*insurance*
autista (m/f)	*driver*
autostrada	*motorway*
batteria	*battery*
benzina	*petrol*
bicicletta	*bicycle*
cambio	*change gear*
camion (m)	*lorry*
candela	*spark plug (R)*
carta (... automobilistica)	*map (road ...)*
carta verde	*green card (R)*
cartello, (... indicatore)	*sign, (direction sign)*
casco	*helmet (R)*
casello (di autostrada)	*tollgate (R)*
cintura di sicurezza	*seat belt*
circolazione vietata	*no through road (R)*
codice della strada (m)	*highway code*
cofano	*bonnet*
controllare	*to control, to check*
copertone (m)	*tyre*
curva; (... a sinistra)	*bend; (left turn)*
dare la precedenza	*to give way*
diritto	*right; straight on*
disco orario	*parking disc (R)*
distributore (di benzina) (m)	*petrol pump*
diversione/deviazione (f)	*diversion*
documenti	*documents (vehicle ...)*
dovere	*duty*
fare	*to make, to do*
filare	*to go*
forare	*to have a puncture (R)*
foratura	*puncture (R)*

frenare	*to brake*
freno	*brake*
frizione	*clutch*
furgone (m)	*van (R)*
gomma	*tyre,*
gonfiare	*to inflate (R)*
gratuito, (ingresso ...)	*free, (admission ...)*
guasto	*breakdown, failure*
guidare	*to drive*
incidente (m)	*accident*
incrocio	*crossroads*
ingorgo	*(traffic) jam (R)*
lavaggio	*washing; car wash*
lavori in corso	*work in progress*
libretto (di circolazione)	*log book (R)*
limite di velocità (m)	*speed limit*
litro	*litre*
macchina	*car*
marca	*make*
moto (cicletta) (f)	*motorcycle*
motore (m)	*engine*
multa	*fine*
nafta	*diesel (R)*
noleggiare	*to hire*
nolo (prendere a ...)	*hire (to ...)*
numero	*number*
olio	*oil*
ore di punta	*rush hours (R)*
panne (in ...)	*breakdown (R)*
parcheggiare	*to park*
parchimetro	*parking meter (R)*
patente (f)	*driving licence*
pedaggio	*toll*
pezzi di ricambio	*spare parts*
pieno; (fare il ...)	*full; (to fill it up)*
pneumatico	*tyre*
Polizia Urbana	*'City Police' (R)*
poliziotto	*policeman*
pompa (di benzina)	*petrol pump*
posteggio	*parking space*
pressione (f)	*pressure*
rallentare	*to slow down*
riparare	*to mend*
ruota	*wheel*
scontro	*bump, collision*
semaforo	*traffic lights*
senso (a ... unico)	*one way*
senza piombo (benzina)	*unleaded (petrol) (R)*

Vocabulary

● ●

sorpassare	*to overtake*
sosta	*parking*
statale (strada ...)	*main road*
super (benzina)	*super, premium fuel*
targa	*number plate*
traffico	*traffic*
veloce	*fast*
velocità	*speed*
verificare	*to check*
vespa	*'vespa', motor scooter*
vigile (urbano) (m)	*'traffic policeman'*
volante (m)	*steering wheel*
vuoto	*empty*

Abbreviations

A Autostrada   *Motorway*
A.C.I. Automobile Club d'Italia *Italian Automobile Club*
A.R. Andata e Ritorno (biglietto di...) *Return ticket*
A.Z. Alitalia   *Italian Airline*
D Diretto   *'Fast Train'*
F.S. Ferrovie dello Stato *State Railways*
FF.SS. Ferrovie dello Stato *State Railways*
MM Metropolitana Milanese *Milan Underground*
SP Strada Provinciale *Provincial Road*
SS Strada Statale   *Main Road*

CC Carabinieri   *'Police Force' (Carabinieri)*
POLFER Polizia Ferroviaria *Railway police*
POLSTRADA Polizia Stradale *Traffic/highway police*
P.S. Pubblica Sicurezza *State Police*
VV.UU Vigili Urbani *'Traffic Police'*

Italian Number Plates: Letters used to indicate provinces

AG	Agrigento	**AL**	Alessandria
AN	Ancona	**AO**	Aosta
AP	Ascoli Piceno	**AQ**	Aquila
AR	Arezzo	**AT**	Asti
AV	Avellino	**BA**	Bari
BG	Bergamo	**BL**	Belluno

BN	Benevento	**BO**	Bologna
BR	Brindisi	**BS**	Brescia
BZ	Bolzano	**CA**	Cagliari
CB	Campobasso	**CE**	Caserta
CH	Chieti	**CL**	Caltanissetta
CN	Cuneo	**CO**	Como
CR	Cremona	**CS**	Cosenza
CT	Catania	**CZ**	Catanzaro
EN	Enna	**FE**	Ferrara
FG	Foggia	**FI**	Firenze
FO	Forlì	**FR**	Frosinone
GE	Genova	**GO**	Gorizia
GR	Grosseto	**IM**	Imperia
IS	Isernia	**LE**	Lecce
LI	Livorno	**LT**	Latina
LU	Lucca	**MC**	Macerata
ME	Messina	**MI**	Milano
MN	Mantova	**MO**	Modena
MS	Massa Carrara	**MT**	Matera
NA	Napoli	**NO**	Novara
NU	Nuoro	**OR**	Oristano
PA	Palermo	**PC**	Piacenza
PD	Padova	**PE**	Pescara
PG	Perugia	**PI**	Pisa
PN	Pordenone	**PR**	Parma
PS	Pesaro	**PT**	Pistoia
PV	Pavia	**PZ**	Potenza
RA	Ravenna	**RC**	Reggio Calabria
RE	Reggio Emilia	**RG**	Ragusa
RI	Rieti	**RO**	Rovigo
SA	Salerno	**SI**	Siena
SO	Sondrio	**SP**	La Spezia
SR	Siracusa	**SS**	Sassari
SV	Savona	**TA**	Taranto
TE	Teramo	**TN**	Trento
TO	Torino	**TP**	Trapani
TR	Terni	**TS**	Trieste
TV	Treviso	**UD**	Udine
VA	Varese	**VC**	Vercelli
VE	Venezia	**VI**	Vicenza
VR	Verona	**VT**	Viterbo
ROMA	Roma		

* * * * *

A.M. Aereonautica Militare *Air Force*
E.I. Esercito Italiano *Italian Army*
M.M. Marina Militare *Navy*
R.M.S. Repubblica di San Marino *Republic of San Marino*

S.C.V. Stato Città del Vaticano
Vatican City
V.F. Vigili del Fuoco *Fire Brigade*

HOLIDAYS

General

abbronzarsi	*to get a tan*
abbronzato	*sun-tanned*
affittare	*to rent, to hire*
agenzia di viaggi	*travel agency*
amare	*to love, to like*
andare	*to go*
andarsene	*to go away*
aria	*air*
asciugamano	*hand-towel*
bagnino	*lifeguard*
bagno	*bathe; bath*
barca	*boat*
benvenuto	*welcome*
calmo	*calm*
campagna	*country-side*
cielo	*sky*
costume da bagno (m)	*bathing costume*
crema solare	*suntan lotion*
di solito	*usually*
diapositiva	*slide, transparency*
dimenticare	*to forget*
durante	*during*
estero (all'...)	*abroad*
estivo	*summer, summery*
ferie	*holidays (R)*
forte	*strong*
foto (f)	*photograph*
galleria	*gallery*
giorno feriale	*working day, week-day (R)*
giorno festivo	*holiday (R)*
giro	*trip*
gita	*excursion; school trip*
gruppo	*group*
guida	*guide*
in macchina	*by car*
insieme, (... a)	*together, (... with)*
interessante	*interesting*
intorno a	*around*

lago	*lake*
lontano da	*far from*
luce (f)	*light*
macchina fotografica	*camera*
mare (m)	*sea*
molto tempo	*a long time*
mondo	*world*
montagna	*mountain*
monumento	*monument*
mosso	*rough*
neve (f)	*snow*
occhiali da sole	*sun-glasses (R)*
ombrellone (m)	*beach umbrella*
ospitalità	*hospitality*
passeggiata	*stroll, walk*
pattinare	*to skate*
piacere	*to please*
pista	*track, piste*
più	*more*
pomeriggio	*afternoon*
preferire	*to prefer*
progetti	*plans*
Pro loco (f)	*'local tourist office'*
prossimo	*next*
pullman (m)	*coach*
qualche volta	*sometimes*
quasi	*almost*
quindici giorni	*fortnight*
quindicina; (... di giorni)	*about fifteen; (a fortnight)*
restare	*to stay*
ricordarsi	*to remember*
rullino/rollino	*film (for camera) (R)*
sabbia	*sand*
sagra	*festival, feast (R)*
salute (f)	*health*
sano	*healthy*
sciare	*to ski*
sedia a sdraio	*deck-chair*
settimana	*week*
sole (m)	*sun*
spiaggia	*beach*
splendere	*to shine*
stagione (f)	*season*
storico	*historic*
sulla riva del mare	*by the sea shore*
tempo	*time, weather*
tramonto	*sunset*

Vocabulary

turismo	*tourism*
turista (m/f)	*tourist*
vacanza	*holiday*
viaggiatore (m)	*traveller*
viaggio	*journey*
villaggio	*village*
visitare	*to visit*
volta	*time*
week-end (m)	*week-end*

Geographical items: *(R)*

Città (Cities):
> Londra (London), Edimburgo (Edinburgh), Parigi (Paris), Bruxelles (Brussels), Strasburgo (Strasbourg), Roma (Rome), Milano (Milan), Torino (Turin), Venezia (Venice), Firenze (Florence) Genova (Genoa), Pisa, Napoli (Naples), ...

Fiumi (Rivers):
> Po, Adige, Tevere (Tiber), Adda, Arno, ...

Montagne (Mountains):
> le Alpi (Alps), gli Appennini (Appennines), ...

Vulcani (Volcanoes):
> Vesuvio (Vesuvius), Stromboli, Vulcano, Etna.

Laghi (Lakes):
> Garda, Maggiore, Como, ...

Mari (Seas):
> il Ligure (Ligurian), il Tirreno (Tyrrhenian), lo Ionio (Ionian), l'Adriatico (Adriatic), il Mediterraneo (the Mediterranean).

Regioni (Regions):
> [North] Valle d'Aosta, Piemonte (Piedmont), Lombardia (Lombardy), Trentino-Alto Adige, Friuli-Venezia Giulia, Veneto, Liguria, Emilia-Romagna; [Centre] Toscana (Tuscany), Marche (The Marches), Umbria, Lazio (Latium), Abruzzo, Molise; [South] Campania, Puglia (Apulia), Basilicata, Calabria; [Islands] Sicilia (Sicily), Sardegna (Sardinia).

Tourist information

(see also Accommodation, Free Time and Entertainment)

a partire da	*starting from*
albergo	*hotel*
andare	*to go*
avere il tempo	*to have time*
ballare	*to dance*
campeggiare	*to camp*
capolavoro	*masterpiece*
cartina geografica	*(small) map*
cercare	*to look for*
certamente	*certainly*
cinema (m)	*cinema*
città	*town, city*
classico	*classic*
comprare	*to buy*
concerto	*concert*
depliant (m)	*leaflet, brochure*
divertente	*amusing*
divertimenti	*amusements*
domandare	*to ask*
fare delle passeggiate	*to go for walks*
generalmente	*generally, usually*
giocare (a tennis ecc.)	*to play (tennis etc.)*
informare	*to inform*
informarsi	*to enquire (about) (R)*
interessarsi	*to be interested in*
moderno	*modern*
museo	*museum*
musica	*music*
negozio	*shop*
opera	*opera*
opuscolo	*booklet, brochure*
parco	*park*
pianta (della città)	*map (of the town)*
presto	*soon*
pubblicità	*advertisement, advertising*

regione (f)	*region, area*
ristorante (m)	*restaurant*
sempre	*always*
spettacolo	*show, performance*
sport (m)	*sport*
teatro	*theatre*
trascorrere	*to pass, to spend*
trovarsi	*to be*
ufficio informazioni	*information office*
volere	*to want*
zoo	*zoo*

Feste	*holidays*
25 aprile	*25th April (Liberation Day)*
Assunzione	*Assumption of the Virgin Mary (15th August)*
Capodanno	*New Year's Day*
Epifania/Befana	*Epiphany (6th January)*
Ferragosto	*Mid-August bank holiday(s)*
I maggio	*1st May (Labour Day)*
Immacolata Concezione	*Immaculate Conception (8th Dec.)*
Lunedì dell'Angelo/di Pasqua	*Easter Monday*
Natale	*Christmas*
Pasqua	*Easter*
Santo Stefano	*Boxing Day (26th December)*
Tutti i Santi/Ognissanti	*All Saints' Day (1st November)*

Abbreviations

A.A.C.S.T./A.S. Azienda Autonoma di Cura, Soggiorno e Turismo *Autonomous Tourist Office*

A.I.G. Associazione Italiana Alberghi per la Gioventù *Italian Youth Hostel Association*

A.P.T. Azienda di Promozione Turistica *Tourist Promotion Board.*

C.A.I. Club Alpino Italiano *Italian Alpine Club*

C.I.T. Compagnia Italiana del Turismo *Italian Tourist Bureau*

E.N.I.T Ente Nazionale Italiano per il Turismo *Italian State Tourist Office*

E.P.T. Ente Provinciale per il Turismo *Provincial Tourist Office*

F.I.C. Federazione Italiana del Campeggio e del Caravanning *Italian Federation of Camping ....*

I.A.T. Informazione e Accoglimento Turistico *Information and Tourist Reception*

s.l.m. sul livello del mare *above sea level*

T.C.I. Touring Club Italiano *Italian Touring Club*

ACCOMMODATION

General

(see also Hotel, Youth Hostel, Camping)

arrivare	*to arrive*
albergo	*hotel*
camera	*room*
caro	*expensive*
comodo	*comfortable*
data	*date*
grande	*large, big*
giorno	*day*
libero	*free*
locanda	*inn (R)*
lontano da	*far*
mandare	*to send*
mezza pensione	*half board (R)*
moderno	*modern*
notte (f)	*night*
partire	*to leave*
passare	*to pass, to spend*
pensione (... completa)	*board (full ...)*
piccolo	*small*
prima colazione	*breakfast*
posto	*place*
per	*for*
potere	*to be able*
presso	*care of, near*

Vocabulary

ringraziare	*to thank*
rispondere	*to reply*
scrivere	*to write*
servire	*to serve*
settimana	*week*
trovarsi	*to be*
vitto e alloggio	*board and lodging (R)*
volere	*to want, to wish*

Hotel

albergo	*hotel*
altro	*other*
apprezzare	*to appreciate*
ascensore (m)	*lift*
bagagli (m, pl.)	*luggage*
camera	*room*
... per due persone	*double ...*
... per una persona	*single ...*
... matrimoniale	*double ...*
... a due letti	*... with twin beds*
... a un letto	*... with a single bed*
... con (il) bagno	*... with a bath*
... con (la) doccia	*... with a shower*
chiamare	*to call (R)*
chiave (f)	*key*
ciascuno	*each*
completo	*full*
compreso, incluso	*inclusive*
conto	*bill, amount*
dettaglio	*detail*
di gran lusso	*luxurious*
direttore (m)	*manager*
direzione (la ...)	*direction, management*
doppia	*double (R)*
entrata	*entrance, hallway*
gabinetti	*toilets*
impiegato	*employee*
lamentarsi	*to complain*
leggero	*light*
lista	*list, menu*
lordo	*gross*
mille	*thousand*
molto	*much*
numero (uno, ecc.)	*number (one, etc.)*
ora	*hour, time*
ospitalità	*hospitality*
padrone (m)	*owner*
pagare	*to pay*

passaporto	*passport*
piano	*floor, storey*
pianterreno	*ground floor*
portare	*to carry, to bring, to take*
premere (il bottone)	*to press (the button) (R)*
prenotare, riservare	*to book, to reserve*
prezzo massimo	*maximum price*
prezzo minimo	*minimum price*
privato	*private*
qualcosa	*something*
quale	*which*
quando	*when*
quanto	*how much*
ricevuta	*receipt (R)*
riservare	*to reserve*
ristorante (m)	*restaurant*
rumore (m)	*noise*
scale	*stairs*
seminterrato	*basement (R)*
senza	*without*
servito	*served*
solamente	*only*
solo	*alone*
svegliare	*to wake (R)*
telefono	*telephone*
televisore (m)	*television set*
trovare	*to find*
uscita di sicurezza	*emergency exit (R)*
valigia	*suitcase*
vista	*view*
visto	*visa*

Youth Hostel (Ostello della Gioventù)

Affittare	*to rent*
aiutare	*to help*
aperto	*open*
bagno	*bathroom*
benvenuto	*welcome*
chiudere	*to close*
chiuso	*closed*
colazione (f)	*breakfast*
completo	*full (R)*
coperta	*blanket*
costare	*to cost*
cucina	*kitchen*
doccia	*shower*
dormire	*to sleep*

69

dormitorio	*dormitory*	coltello	*knife*
gabinetti	*toilets*	**corda**	*cord, rope*
giorno	*day*	cucchiaio	*spoon*
letto	*bed*	**dispensa portatile**	*food box*
mappa	*map*	elettrico	*electric*
ospite (m/f)	*guest*	fiammiferi	*matches*
pagare	*to pay*	forchetta	*fork*
paio, (un ... di lenzuola)	*pair, (a ... of sheets)*	fornello a spirito/gas	*spirit /gas stove*
pasto	*meal*	freddo	*cold*
pasto pronto	*ready to eat meal*	gabinetti	*toilets*
pattumiera	*dustbin*	**griglia (alla ...)**	*grilled*
per giorno (persona, notte)	*per day (person, night)*	lampada a gas	*gas lamp*
posta	*mail*	lavabo	*wash basin*
pranzare	*to have lunch*	lavare	*to wash*
prenotare	*to book, to reserve*	lavatrice (f)	*washing machine*
quanto	*how much*	**mazzuolo**	*mallet*
sacco a pelo	*sleeping bag*	municipale	*municipal, of the town*
sala giochi	*games room, amusement arcade*	**nodo**	*knot*
sala da pranzo	*dining room*	**picchetto**	*tent-peg*
salvo	*except*	**pila**	*battery; 'torch'*
silenzio	*silence*	posizione (f)	*position, situation*
singola	*single*	preparare	*to prepare*
soggiorno	*stay; living room*	**presa (di corrente)**	*socket*
tariffa	*price list, charge*	**pulito**	*clean*
tutto l'anno	*all year round*	**regolamento**	*regulations (R)*
ufficio	*office*	roulotte (f)	*caravan*
vacanza	*holiday*	sacco per i rifiuti	*rubbish bag (R)*
volere	*to want*	**seggiolino, (... pieghevole)**	*stool, (folding stool)*
		settimana	*week*
Camping		**spina (elettrica)**	*(electric) plug*
		sporco	*dirty*
accettare	*to accept*	supplemento	*supplement*
acqua (non) potabile	*(non) drinking water*	**tavola pieghevole**	*folding table*
adulto	*adult*	tenda	*tent*
aiutare	*to help*	termos (m)	*thermos flask*
albero	*tree*	terreno	*ground*
bicchiere (m)	*beaker, glass*	torcia elettrica	*(electric) torch*
borraccia	*water bottle*	veicolo	*vehicle*
branda	*camp bed*	**veranda**	*verandah*
bussola	*compass*	**zaino**	*ruck-sack*
caldo	*hot*		
campeggiare	*to camp*		
campeggiatore (m)	*camper*		
campeggio; (andare in ...)	*camping site; (to go camping)*		
cercare	*to look for*		

Vocabulary

FOOD AND DRINK

General

aceto	vinegar
acqua minerale	mineral water
affatto	at all
affumicato	smoked
altrettanto	and the same to you
anche	also
antipasto (misto)	hors d'oeuvre (mixed)
apparecchiare	to lay the table
appetitoso	appetizing (R)
aranciata	orangeade
arrosto	roast
augurare	to wish
ben cotto	well cooked
bene	well
benvenuto	welcome
bere	to drink
bevanda	drink
bibita	(soft) drink
birra	beer
biscotto	biscuit
boccone (m)	bite, mouthful
brindare	to toast (R)
brioche (f)	'brioche', 'bun'
brodo; (riso in ...)	broth; (rice soup)
buon appetito	enjoy your meal
buono	good, nice
burro	butter
caffellatte (m)	white coffee
caffettiera	coffee pot, coffee-maker
caffè (m)	coffee
caldo	hot
cannelloni	cannelloni
cappuccino	cappuccino
caramelle	sweets
casa; (fatto in ....)	house; (home made)
cattivo	bad
cena	dinner; supper
cenare	to dine
chiedere	to ask for
cibo	food
cincin!	cheers!
cioccolata	chocolate
coca-cola	coca-cola
colazione (prima ...) (f)	breakfast

coltello	knife
come	as, how
compere	shopping
crema	cream; custard
crostata	tart (R)
cucchiaino	teaspoon
cucchiaio	spoon
cuoco	cook
delizioso	delicious
detestare	to detest, to hate
di solito	usually
dolce, dessert (m)	sweet, dessert
dozzina (mezza ...)	dozen (half ...)
far colazione	to have breakfast; to have lunch
fare	to make, to do
fetta	slice
filoncino	long loaf
forchetta	fork
formaggio	cheese
forno; (al ...)	oven; baked
freddo	cold
fresco	fresh, cool
frittata	omelet
frittella	fritter (R)
fritto	fried
galletta	cracker, biscuit
gassosa	fizzy lemonade (R)
gelato	ice cream
ghiacciato	frozen, ice-cold
grazie	thank you
gusto	taste
lasagne (f, pl.)	lasagna
latte (m)	milk
limonata	lemonade
liquore; (liquori) (m)	liqueur; liquor; (spirits)
maccheroni	macaroni
macedonia	fruit salad
maionese (f)	mayonnaise
mangiare	to eat
marmellata	marmalade, jam
Marsala	Marsala
Martini (m)	Martini
mensa	canteen, refectory (R)
merenda	(afternoon) snack
metà	half
mi piace, (non ...)	I like, I don't like

Vocabulary

minestra	soup	teiera	teapot
minestrina	thin soup, broth	tè (m)	tea
minestrone (m)	minestrone, vegetable soup	tipico (piatto ...)	typical dish
		torta	cake
molto	much, a lot of	uovo	egg
mozzarella	'mozzarella'	vaniglia	vanilla
olio di semi	vegetable oil	vassoio	tray (R)
ora	now	**vermut (m)**	vermouth
padella	frying pan	vino (bianco, rosso, rosè)	wine (white, red, rosé)
pagnotta	round loaf		
pane (m)	bread	yoghurt (m)	yoghurt
passare	to purée, to strain	**zuccherato**	sweetened; sugared
pasta	pasta; pastry	zucchero	sugar
pasticceria	pastry shop, 'patisserie', cakes	**zuppa inglese**	'trifle'
		zuppa	soup

pasto	meal
patate fritte	chips, French fries
patatine	potato crisps
pentola	pot
per cortesia	please
pezzo	piece, a bit
piattino	saucer
piatto	plate; dish
piccante	spicy, hot
picnic (m)	picnic
pietanza	course; dish
pizza	pizza
pranzare	to lunch
preferire	to prefer
prendere	to take, to have
preparare	to prepare, to make
provare	to try
provvista	supply, stock
ravioli	ravioli
ricetta	recipe
riso	rice
salato	salty, salt (adj)
sale (m)	salt
salute (alla ...!)	cheers! good health!
sapore (m)	flavour, taste
spaghetti	spaghetti
specie di	type of
spremuta	fresh fruit juice
squisito	exquisite, delicious
succo di frutta	fruit juice
tagliare	to cut
tagliatelle	tagliatelle
tavola	table
tazza	cup

Café, Restaurant and other Public Places

a puntino (cotto a ...)	cooked to a turn
accomodarsi	to take a seat, to come in
acqua	water
al dente	'firm to the bite'
ancora	again, more
apprezzare	to appreciate
approvare	to approve
aver fame, sete	to be hungry, thirsty
aver vergogna di	to be ashamed of
aver voglia di	to feel like
bar (m)	bar, café; cocktail cabinet
bicchiere (m)	glass
birra	beer
boccale (m)	jug (R)
bottiglia	bottle
caffè (m)	coffee; coffee house, café, bar
cameriere (m)	waiter
capocuoco	chef (R)
caraffa	carafe, decanter
carta; (... dei vini, alla ...)	menu; (wine list, à la carte)
club (m)	club
come	how, as
completamente	completely
complimentarsi	to compliment, to congratulate
complimenti!	Well done! Congratulations!
consigliare	to recommend
contento	happy, satisfied

Vocabulary

conto	bill	pizzeria	'pizzeria'
contorno	vegetables, side dish	**poco cotto**	underdone
coperto	cover charge	**portare**	to carry, to bring, to take
cornetto	'croissant', 'cornetto'	**posto**	place, seat
costare	to cost	**prenotare**	to book
cotoletta	cutlet, chop	primo (piatto)	first (course)
cucina	kitchen; cooking	**protestare**	to complain, to protest
dare	to give	**quale**	which, what
desiderare	to want, to wish	quanto	how much
dove	where	quarto, (un ... di vino)	quarter, (a ... litre of wine)
eccellente	excellent		
errore (m)	error, mistake	regionale	regional, local
esattamente	exactly, precisely	ristorante (m)	restaurant
espresso	espresso (coffee)	saporito	tasty
fa lo stesso	it's the same	**sbaglio**	mistake, error
fiasco	flask	scegliere	to choose
frizzante	fizzy, sparkling (R)	**scelta**	selection, choice
gabinetto	toilet	scontrino	receipt
ghiaccio	ice	secondo (piatto)	second (course)
giusto	right, fair	servire	to serve
gradire	to enjoy, to like	servizio	service, service charge
griglia (alla ...)	grilled (R)	signore, signora	Sir, Madam
in più	more, extra	**soddisfatto**	satisfied, pleased
inammissibile	inadmissible, intolerable	solo	only, alone
incluso/compreso	included	speciale; (è ...)	special; (it is delicious)
insultare	to insult	specialità	speciality
interamente	entirely, completely	specie, (una ... di ...)	type, (a type/kind of ...)
irritarsi	to get angry, to get annoyed	**spumante** (m)	'sparkling wine'
		supplemento	supplement, extra portion, extra charge
lamentarsi	to complain		
lesso	boiled meat (R)	tavola calda	snack bar, hot lunch counter
litro	litre		
locale (m)	place, premises	tavolo	table
malato	ill	telefono	telephone
male di stomaco	stomach ache	**tipo**	type, kind
mancia	tip	tovaglia	table cloth
menu/menù (m)	menu	tovagliolo	napkin
mezzo	half	trattoria	(small) restaurant, inn, 'trattoria'
nessuno	no-one, nobody, none		
netto	net, clear	**troppo cotto**	overdone
offrire	to offer	trovare	to find
ordinare	to order	turistico (menù ...)	fixed-price menu
ordine (m)	order	un po'	a bit, a little
padrone (m)	owner	**vario, (varie volte)**	varied, various, (several times)
panino; (... imbottito)	roll; (filled roll, sandwich)		
		vegetariano	vegetarian
per piacere/favore	please	**vergognarsi**	to be ashamed
persona	person	voglio, (non ...)	I want, (I don't ...)
piatto (del giorno)	dish (of the day)	vorrei	I'd like

Fruit and vegetables

aglio	garlic
albicocca	apricot
ananas (m)	pineapple
anguria	water melon (R)
arancia	orange
banana	banana
carciofo	artichoke
carota	carrot
cavolfiore (m)	cauliflower
cavolo	cabbage
cetriolo	cucumber
ciliegia	cherry
cipolla	onion
fagioli	beans
fagiolini	string beans, French beans
fragola	strawberry
frutta	fruit
fungo	mushroom
insalata; (... mista/russa)	salad, lettuce; (mixed/Russian salad)
lampone (m)	raspberry
limone (m)	lemon
mela	apple
melanzana	aubergine (R)
melone (m)	melon
oliva	olive
patata	potato
pepe (m)	pepper
peperone; (... rosso/verde)	pepper; (red/green ...)
pera	pear
pesca	peach
piselli	peas
pomodoro	tomato
pompelmo	grapefruit (R)
porro	leek
sedano	celery
uva (f, sing.)	grapes
verdura (f, sing.)	vegetables, greens
zucchino	courgette

Meat and Fish

agnello	lamb
aragosta	lobster (R)
baccalà (m)	dried salted cod (R)

bistecca, (... ai ferri)	steak, (grilled ...)
bollito	boiled meat (R)
capretto	kid (R)
coniglio	rabbit (R)
cozze	mussels
frittura di pesce	mixed fried fish
frutti di mare (m, pl.)	seafood
gamberetti grigi/rossi	shrimps/prawns
granchio	crab (R)
maiale (m)	pork
manzo	beef
merluzzo	cod (R)
montone (m)	mutton
mortadella	'mortadella'
ostrica	oyster (R)
pesce (m)	fish
pollo	chicken
prosciutto (crudo/cotto)	ham (cured/cooked)
salame (m)	salami
salmone (m)	salmon
sardina	sardine
scampi	scampi
sogliola	sole
tacchino	turkey
tonno	tuna
trota	trout
vitello	veal
vongola	clam

SHOPPING

General

(See also Food and Drink)

a buon mercato	cheap
a partire da	starting from (R)
abbastanza	enough, rather
accettare	to accept
agenzia di cambio	Bureau de change
aiutare	to help
altro	other
andare, (... a cercare)	to go. (... and look for)
aperto	open
aprire	to open
ascensore (m)	lift
assaggiare	to taste (R)

Vocabulary

● ●

assai/molto	*very*
assegno turistico	*travellers' cheque*
aumentare	*to increase*
aumento	*increase*
aver bisogno di	*to need*
avere	*to have*
banca	*bank*
banconota	*banknote*
barattolo; (... di latta)	*jar,pot; (tin)*
basta così, grazie	*that's enough, thank you*
biglietto da diecimila lire	*ten thousand lire note*
bilancio	*balance, budget*
borsa	*bag*
bottega/negozio	*shop*
bottiglia	*bottle*
busta	*envelope*
c'è, ci sono	*there is, there are*
cambiare	*to change*
cambio	*exchange*
caro	*dear, expensive*
carrello	*trolley*
carta da lettere	*writing paper*
carta di credito	*credit card*
carta	*paper*
cartolina (postale)	*postcard*
cassa	*cash desk*
cerino	*(waxed) match*
cestino	*basket*
che cosa?	*what?*
chilo	*kilogramme*
chiudere	*to close, to shut*
cliente (m/f)	*customer*
commerciante (m/f)	*trader, shopkeeper*
commesso	*shop-assistant*
compilare	*to compile, to fill in*
comprare	*to buy*
compreso	*included*
contare	*to count*
conto	*bill, account*
corto	*short*
cosa	*thing*
costare	*to cost*
costoso	*expensive, dear*
credito	*credit*
cristalleria	*crystal-ware*
da parte (mettere ...)	*to put aside*
dare	*to give*

deodorante (m)	*deodorant*
desidera?	*can I help you?*
desiderare	*to wish, to want*
differente	*different*
differenza	*difference*
disco	*disc, record*
dispiacere	*to dislike, to regret, to be sorry*
documento (di riconoscimento)	*document (identity ...)*
domandare	*to ask*
dozzina	*dozen*
è tutto?	*is that all?*
eccetto	*except*
errore (m)	*mistake*
esatto	*exact*
essere	*to be*
etto	*100 grammes*
fare la spesa	*to do the shopping*
farsi prestare	*to borrow*
ferie (f, pl.)	*holidays (R)*
fetta	*slice*
fiammifero	*match*
firmare	*to sign*
non funziona	*out of order*
garanzia	*guarantee*
giocattolo	*toy*
gioielleria	*jeweller's (shop)*
gioiello	*jewel*
giornale (m)	*newspaper*
gradire	*to appreciate; to like*
grande	*large; big*
gratuito	*free (of charge) (R)*
grazie	*thank you*
guadagnare	*to earn*
guida	*guide*
I.V.A	*Value Added Tax (R)*
importato	*imported (R)*
imposta	*tax; duty*
incluso	*included*
istruzioni; (... per l'uso)	*instructions; (directions for use)*
lamentarsi	*to complain*
largo	*large; broad*
latte (m)	*milk*
lavorare	*to work*
leggero	*light*
libretto d'assegni	*cheque book*

libro	book	porcellana	porcelain, china
lira	lira	portare	to carry; to wear
lista/elenco	list	**povero**	poor
lungo	long	preferire	to prefer
magazzino	store, shop	prego!	don't mention it!, you are welcome!
mancare	to lack		
matita	pencil	prendere	to take
meglio	better, best	**prestare**	to lend
meno; (un po'...)	less; (a bit ...)	prezzo, (... fisso)	price, (fixed ...)
mercato	market	primo	first
mese (m)	month	profumo	perfume
metà	half	provare	to try
mettere	to put; to wear	qualche	some, a few
mezzo	half	**qualcosa**	something
migliore	better, best	quale	which
milione (m)	million	qualità	quality
mille	thousand	**quantità**	quantity
misura	size	quanto, (... fa?)	how much, (... is it?)
moda	fashion	**reclamo**	complaint
modello	model	regalo	present
modulo	form	reparto	department (R)
molto	much, a lot	resto	change
moneta	coin	ricco	rich
mostrare	to show	**ricevere**	to receive
naturale	natural	**ricevuta**	receipt
negoziante (m/f)	shopkeeper	ricordo	souvenir
normale	normal	riduzione (f)	reduction
nuovo	new	**rimborsare**	to pay back (R)
offrire	to offer	**rimborso**	refund
ombrello	umbrella	ringraziare	to thank
orologio	watch	risparmiare	to save
pacchetto	(small) packet, parcel	**ritornare**	to return
pacco	parcel	rivista	magazine
pagamento	payment	rotto	broken
pagare	to pay	**rullino/rollino**	film (for camera)
paio	pair	sacchetto	(small) bag
parecchio	quite a lot of	saldi	sales
passaporto	passport	sbagliato	wrong, mistaken
penna	pen	**sbaglio**	mistake
per piacere	please	**scaffale (m)**	shelf
però	but, however	**scala mobile**	escalator
pesante	heavy	scatola	box
pezzo	piece	scelta	choice, selection
piacere	to like	sconto	discount
piano, (primo ...)	floor, (first ...)	**seminterrato**	basement
pianterreno	ground floor	settimana	week
piccolo	small	**shampoo (m)**	shampoo
poco	little; not much	soldi (m, pl.)	money

Vocabulary

• •

sopra	on, over, above
sostituire	to substitute, to change (R)
sotto	under
spendere	to spend
spesa; (fare la ...)	shopping; (to do the shopping)
spiccioli (m, pl.)	small money, change
sport (m)	sport
sterlina	pound (sterling)
stesso	same
supplemento	extra charge
svendita	(clearance) sale
tabaccaio	tobacconist
tascabile; (dizionario ...)	pocket; (... dictionary)
tassa	tax, duty
tempo libero	free time
travellers' cheque (m)	travellers' cheque
troppo	too, too much
trovare	to find
trucco	make-up
tutto	all
ufficio	office
uso	use
va bene	all right
vale	it is worth
valore (m)	value, price
vendere	to sell
vendita (in ...)	for sale
vergognarsi	to be ashamed
vero	real, genuine (R)
vetrina	shop window
volere	to want
vorrei	I'd like

Shops

abbigliamento (negozio di ...)	clothes shop
alimentari (negozio di ...)	grocer's (shop)
cartoleria	stationery (shop)
centro commerciale	shopping centre
drogheria	grocer's (shop)
edicola	newspaper kiosk (R)
farmacia	pharmacy; chemist's (shop)
fioraio	florist
fruttivendolo	greengrocer's (shop)

gelateria	ice-cream (shop)
gioielleria	jeweller's (shop)
giornalaio	newsagent
grande magazzino	department store
latteria	dairy
lavanderia	laundry
lavasecco/lavanderia a secco	dry-cleaner's (shop) (R)
libreria	bookshop
macelleria	butcher's (shop)
mercato	market
panetteria/fornaio	baker's (shop)
parrucchiere (m)	hairdresser
pasticceria	confectioner's (shop)
pastificio	pasta factory (R)
pescheria	fishmonger's (shop) (R)
profumeria	perfumer's shop
rosticceria	roast meat shop, 'rôtisserie'
salumeria	delicatessen (shop)
supermercato	supermarket
tabaccheria	tobacconist's (shop)
tintoria	dry-cleaner's (shop) (R)

Clothes

abbigliamento; (un negozio d'...)	clothes; (a ... shop)
allargare (i pantaloni)	to let out (the trousers) (R)
allungare (il vestito)	to lengthen (the dress) (R)
bikini (m)	bikini
blusa/camicetta	blouse
calze	socks, stockings
calzini	socks
calzoni	trousers
camicia	shirt
cappello	hat
cappotto	(over) coat
cintura	belt
collant, (un paio di ...)	tights, (a pair of ...)
costume da bagno (m)	bathing costume
cravatta	tie
fazzoletto	handkerchief
giacca a vento	wind cheater; anorak
giacca	jacket
gonna	skirt

77

• •

impermeabile (m)	*raincoat*
jeans (m, pl.)	*jeans*
maglia	*jersey*
pantaloni, (paio di ...)	*trousers, (pair of ...)*
pigiama (m)	*pyjamas*
pullover (m)	*pullover*
sandali	*sandals*
scarpa	*shoe*
soprabito	*overcoat*
stivale (m)	*boot*
stoffa	*cloth, material*
strappato (un vestito ....)	*a torn dress*
stretto	*tight*
stringere (la giacca)	*to take in (the jacket) (R)*
taglia	*size*
tasca	*pocket (R)*
vestiti/abiti	*clothes*
vestito	*suit, dress*

Weights and measurements

abbastanza	*enough*
leggero	*light*
mezzo	*half*
pesante	*heavy*
pesare	*to weigh*
peso, (...netto)	*weight, (net ...)*

cg	**centigrammo**	*centigramme*
g	grammo	*gramme*
hg	**ettogrammo**	*hectogramme*
kg	chilogrammo	*kilogramme*
q	quintale	*quintal, 100 kg*
t	**tonnellata**	*tonne , 1,000 kg*

ml	**millilitro**	*millilitre*
cl	**centilitro**	*centilitre*
l	litro	*litre*

mm	**millimetro**	*millimetre*
cm	centimetro	*centimetre*
m	metro	*metre*
km	chilometro	*kilometre*

Materials

argento	*silver*
carta	*paper*
cotone (m)	*cotton*
ferro	*iron*
lana	*wool*
legno	*wood*
metallo	*metal*
nailon	*nylon*
oro	*gold*
pelle	*leather*
plastica	*plastic*
seta	*silk*
stoffa	*cloth, material*
velluto	*velvet*
vetro	*glass*

Colours

arancione	*orange*
azzurro	*azure, light blue*
bianco	*white*
celeste	*light blue*
chiaro	*light*
colore	*colour*
giallo	*yellow*
grigio	*grey*
marrone	*brown*
nero	*black*
rosa	*pink*
rosso	*red*
scuro	*dark*
verde	*green*
viola	*violet*

SERVICES

Post Office & Telephone

all'estero	*abroad*
ascoltare	*to listen*
attimo	*moment*
bene	*well*
bolletta	*bill (R)*
buca/cassetta delle lettere	*letter box*
busta	*envelope*

Vocabulary

• •

cabina (telefonica)	*telephone box (R)*
carta telefonica	*phone-card*
cartolina (postale)	*postcard*
centralino	*telephone exchange (R)*
centralinista (m/f)	*operator (R)*
chi parla?	*who is speaking?*
chiamare	*to call*
chiamata telefonica	*telephone call*
corrispondenza	*correspondence, mail*
da parte di	*on behalf of*
destinatario	*addressee (R)*
elenco telefonico	*telephone directory (R)*
fare il numero	*to dial the number*
fare uno sbaglio	*to make a mistake*
fermo posta	*poste restante*
fessura	*slot*
foglio	*page, sheet*
fragile	*fragile (R)*
francobollo	*stamp*
fuori servizio	*out of service (R)*
gettone (m)	*(telephone) token*
guasto	*out of order*
impostare/imbucare	*to post*
indirizzo	*address*
interno	*extension*
introdurre	*to insert (R)*
l'altro ieri	*the day before yesterday*
lettera	*letter*
levata	*collection (R)*
libero	*free*
male	*bad*
mandare	*to send*
mittente (m/f)	*sender (R)*
modulo	*form*
moneta	*coin*
non funziona	*does not work*
numero	*number*
occupato	*engaged*
pacchetto (postale)	*(small) parcel*
pacco	*parcel*
Pagine Gialle	*Yellow Pages*
parlare	*to talk*
posta	*mail*
posta aerea	*air mail*
Posta Centrale	*General Post Office*
postino/portalettere	*postman (R)*
prefisso	*area code (telephone)*
pronto!	*hallo!*

qua, qui	*here*
quando	*when*
quanto costa?	*how much is it?*
quanto	*how much*
raccomandata, (fare un ...)	*registered letter, (to send a ...)*
restituzione (delle monete)	*returned (coins) (R)*
riagganciare (il ricevitore)	*to hang up (R)*
ricevere	*to receive*
richiamare	*to call back (R)*
riempire/compilare	*to fill in*
Sali e Tabacchi	*tobacconist's (shop)*
segnale (m)	*signal*
segreteria telefonica	*answerphone (R)*
sentire	*to hear*
sganciare	*to lift up the receiver (R)*
spedire	*to send*
suonare	*to ring*
tabaccheria	*tobacconist's (shop)*
tariffa (postale)	*rates (postal), postage*
telefonare	*to telephone*
telefono	*telephone*
telegramma (m)	*telegram*
ufficio postale	*post office*
urbana/interurbana (telefonata ...)	*local/ long distance call (R)*
urgente	*urgent*
vaglia (m)	*postal order (R)*

Abbreviations

all.	Allegato	*Enclosed*
C.A.P.	Codice di Avviamento Postale	*Post code*
c.a.	Corrente anno.	*Of this year*
c.c.p.	Conto Corrente Postale	*Current Postal Account*
c/o	Presso	*Care of*
c.m.	Corrente mese	*Of this month*
C.P.	Casella Postale	*Post Office Box*
Ns; n/	Nostro	*Our*
P.T.	Poste e Telegrafi	*Post and Telegraph*
PP.TT.	Poste e Telecomunicazioni	*Post & Telecommunications*
S.I.P.	Società Italiana per l'Esercizio Telefonico	*Italian Telephone Service*

V., V/ Vostro — *Your*
Vs.; Vs/ Vostra lettera *Your letter*

c.so Corso — *Main Street, Avenue*
P.za Piazza — *Square*
Prov. Provincia — *Province*
V.le Viale — *Avenue*
V. Via — *Street, Road*

Sig. Signore — *Mr.*
Sig.ra Signora — *Mrs.*
Sig.na Signorina — *Miss*
Egr. Sig. Egregio Signore *Dear Sir*
Gent. Sig.ra. Gentile Signora *Dear Mrs.*
Dott. Dottore — *Dr.*
Dott.ssa Dottoressa *Dr.*
Mitt. Mittente — *Sender*
Prof. Professore — *Professor, Teacher*
Prof.ssa. Professor *Teacher*

Bank or Exchange Office

accettare — *to accept*
agenzia di cambio *exchange bureau*
assegno (bancario) *cheque (R)*
banca — *bank*
banconota — *banknote*
biglietto da diecimila lire *ten thousand lire note*
cambiare — *to change*
cambio (corso del ...) *exchange, rate of exchange*
carta assegni — *cheque card*
carta di credito — *credit card*
cassa — *cash desk, till*
cassa continua — *night safe*
Cassa di Risparmio *(Savings) Bank (R)*
commissione (f) — *commission*
conto corrente — *current account*
denaro — *money*
documento di riconoscimento *proof of identity*
firmare — *to sign*
girare — *to endorse*
interesse (m) — *interest*
istituto di credito *bank (R)*
libretto di assegni *cheque book*
lira — *lira*

modulo — *form*
moneta — *coin (R)*
passaporto — *passport*
per cento — *per cent*
prestito — *loan*
ritirare — *to withdraw*
saldo — *settlement, balance (R)*
soldi (m, pl.) — *money*
spiccioli (m, pl.) — *small change*
sportello; (... automatico) *counter; (cash point)*
sterlina — *pound (sterling) (R)*
travellers' cheque *travellers' cheque (R)*
ufficio di cambio *bureau de change*
valore — *value*
valuta — *currency (R)*

Abbreviations

c/c Conto Corrente. *Current Account*
C.E.E. Comunità Economica Europea *E.E.C. European Economic Community*
I.C.E. Istituto per il Commercio Estero *Foreign Trade Institute*
I.V.A. Imposta sul Valore Aggiunto *Value Added Tax (V.A.T.)*
S.p.A. Società per Azioni *Joint-stock company*
S.r.l. Società a responsabilità limitata *Limited Company (Ltd)*
L.it Lire italiane *Italian Lire*
L.st. Lire sterline *Pound (sterling)*

Lost Property

accusare — *to accuse*
argento — *silver*
arrabbiato — *angry*
bianco — *white*
bicicletta — *bicycle*
bisogna — *need, it is necessary*
borsa, (borsetta) *bag, (hand-bag)*
borsellino — *purse*
braccialetto — *bracelet*
carta d'identità — *identity card*
cercare — *to look for*
certo — *certain*

Vocabulary

chiaro	clear, light	misura	size
chiave (f)	key	modulo	form
cinepresa	cine-camera	moto (f)	motor-bike
cognome (m)	surname	nero	black
collana	necklace	nessuno	no-one
colore (m)	colour	nuovo di zecca	brand new (R)
come	as, like	nuovo	new
consolato	consulate	oggi	today
contento	pleased	ombrello	umbrella
dappertutto	everywhere	oro	gold
data	date	orologio	watch
dentro	inside	ovunque	everywhere
descritto	described	passaporto	passport
descrizione (f)	description	peccato (che ...!)	what a pity!
di sopra	upstairs (R)	pelle (f)	leather
di sotto	downstairs (R)	perdere	to lose
dimenticare	to forget	pieno	full
Dio mio!	my God!	plastica	plastic
dispiaciuto	sorry; annoyed	pomeriggio	afternoon
diverso	different	portafoglio	wallet
documenti (personali)	(identification)	possibile	possible
	papers	prima	before
dopo	after	provare	to try
dove	where	quando	when
dovere	duty, to have to	quello	that (one)
dubitare	to doubt	questo	this (one)
fino a	as far as, until	restituire	to give back
firmare	to sign	rettangolare	rectangular
flash (m)	flash (light)	ricompensa	reward
forma	shape	riconoscere	to recognise
formidabile	formidable	ricordarsi	to remember
fortunato	lucky, fortunate	ritrovare	to find
furioso	furious	rotondo	round
furto	theft	rubare	to steal
grande	big, large	sapere	to know
ieri, (l'altro ...)	yesterday, (the day before ...)	scoprire	to discover
		scuro	dark
impossibile	impossible	sfortunato	unfortunate, unlucky
ladro; (al ...!)	burglar, pickpocket; (stop thief!)	simile	similar, like
		sorprendersi	to be surprised
largo	large	statura	height
lasciare	to leave	stretto	narrow
libretto degli assegni	cheque book	tasca	pocket
lungo	long	trovare	to find
macchina fotografica	camera	ufficio oggetti smarriti	lost property office
marca	make	uguale	equal; like
mattino/mattina	morning	valigia	suit case
medio	medium, average	vecchio	old
metallo	metal	vuoto	empty

81

zaino	ruck-sack

Having things repaired or cleaned

accettare	to accept
aggiustare	to mend
ago	needle (R)
auto-stop (fare l'...)	to hitch-hike
autorimessa	garage
batteria	battery
bene	well
bisogna	it is necessary
bottone (m)	button
buco	hole
cadere	to fall
calzolaio	cobbler, shoe-repair shop
cambiare	to change
camminare	to walk
capace	able
cattivo	bad
controllare/verificare	to check
cucire	to sew
dispiaciuto	displeased, sorry
domani	tomorrow
dopodomani	the day after tomorrow
dovere	duty, to have to
duro	hard
elettricista (m)	electrician
fare	to make, to do
filo	cotton thread (R)
fissare	to fix
flash (m)	flash (light)
freno	brake
funzionare	to work
garantire	to guarantee (R)
gentile	kind
guastarsi	to break, to fail
guasto	out of order; breakdown
idraulico	plumber
impossibile	impossible
imprestare/prestare	to lend
in questo caso	in this case
iniziare	to begin
investire	to collide with
lavaggio; (... automatico/a mano)	washing; (automatic/hand car wash) (R)
lavanderia (automatica)	launderette
lavatura a secco	dry cleaning
lavandino	sink
lavare	to wash
lavatrice (f)	washing machine
mamma mia!	goodness gracious!
marca	make (R)
marce	gears
meccanico	mechanic
motore (m)	engine
naturalmente	of course
non ne vale la pena	it is not worth it
nonostante	in spite of
perdita	leak
possibile	possible
prego!	don't mention it!
prendere in prestito	to borrow
promettere	to promise
pronto	ready
proporre	to propose
provare	to try
pulire	to clean
pulito	clean
quanto tempo	how long
raccomandare	to recommend
radiatore (m)	radiator
reclamare	to complain
rendere	to give back, to return
ricambio; (pezzo di ...)	replacement; (spare part)
ricevuta	receipt
rifiutare	to refuse
rimborsare	to refund
ringraziare	to thank
riparare	to repair
ritornare	to return
rompersi	to break
rotto	broken
rumore (m)	noise
ruota di scorta	spare wheel (R)
scoppiato	burst
soddisfatto	satisfied
sporco	dirty
stato	state, condition
strano	strange
suggerire	to suggest
svendita	sale
tra due ore	in two hours
velocità	speed
vergognarsi	to be ashamed

Vocabulary

HEALTH AND WELFARE

General

aiuto	*help*
aver mal di denti	*to have a tooth ache*
gola	*sore throat*
schiena	*back ache*
stomaco	*stomach ache*
testa	*head ache*
ammalarsi	*to fall ill*
ammalato	*ill*
andare (a letto)	*to go (to bed)*
asciugamano	*hand/face towel*
asciugarsi	*to dry (oneself)*
bene	*well*
bocca	*mouth*
braccio	*arm*
caldo	*hot, warm*
capelli (m, pl.)	*hair*
caviglia	*ankle*
coricarsi	*to go to bed; to lie down*
cuore (m)	*heart*
dentifricio	*tooth-paste*
dito	*finger*
dormire	*to sleep*
fame (f)	*hunger*
fare il bagno	*to have a bath*
fare la doccia	*to have a shower*
farsi la barba	*to shave*
fegato	*liver*
forse	*perhaps*
fragile	*fragile, weak*
freddo	*cold*
gamba	*leg*
ginocchio	*knee*
lavarsi	*to wash*
letto	*bed*
lingua	*tongue*
malato	*ill*
mano (f)	*hand*
normale	*normal*
occhio	*eye*
orecchio	*ear*
osso	*bone*
pelle (f)	*skin*
pericoloso	*dangerous*

piede (m)	*foot*
preoccupazione (f)	*worry, concern*
pulito	*clean*
rasoio	*razor*
rilassarsi	*to relax*
salute (f)	*health*
sangue (m)	*blood*
sapone (m)	*soap*
sciampo/shampoo	*shampoo*
sete (f)	*thirst*
spalla	*shoulder*
sporco	*dirty*
stanco	*tired*
stare meglio	*to be better*
va bene	*it is all right, fine*

Illness and injury

ambulanza	*ambulance*
ambulatorio	*consulting room, surgery*
annegare	*to drown*
ansioso	*anxious*
appuntamento	*appointment*
armadietto dei medicinali	*medicine cabinet*
aspirina	*aspirin*
assicurato	*insured*
assicurazione (f)	*insurance*
attacco	*fit, stroke, attack*
benda	*bandage*
bisogna	*it is necessary (R)*
bruciarsi la mano	*to burn one's hand*
cadere	*to fall*
cancro	*cancer*
cerotto (adesivo)	*(sticking) plaster*
clinica	*clinic*
colpo di sole	*sunstroke*
compressa	*tablet (R)*
consigliare	*to advise*
contro	*against*
cotone idrofilo	*cotton-wool (R)*
crisi (f, sing.)	*attack*
cucchiaiata	*spoonful*
dentista (m/f)	*dentist*
diarrea	*diarrhoea*
dieta	*diet*
dolore (m)	*pain*

●●●

dopo	after	prima	before, first
dottore (m)	doctor	problema (m)	problem
dovere	duty, to have to	pronto soccorso	first aid
è necessario	it is necessary (R)	puntura	injection (R)
essere ammesso	to be admitted	qualche cosa	something
farmacia	chemist's (shop)	raffreddato (essere ...)	to have a cold
farmacista (m/f)	chemist	ricetta	prescription
far male	to hurt	rimedio	remedy
farsi male	to hurt oneself	riposarsi	to rest
fascia	bandage	rompersi il braccio (ecc.)	to break one's arm (etc.)
fasciatura	dressing, bandages		
febbre (f)	fever, high temperature	salute (f)	health
febbre da fieno	hay fever	sanguinare	to bleed
ferito	wounded	sciroppo	syrup, mixture
fresco	fresh	sentirsi	to feel
giorno	day	sofferente	suffering, ill
grave	serious	soffrire	to suffer
gravemente	gravely, seriously	stare male	to feel ill
guarire	to recover	stare peggio	to be worse
incendio	fire	tagliarsi	to cut
indigestione (f)	indigestion	tosse (f)	cough
influenza	infuenza	tubetto	tube
ingessare	to put in plaster	vedere	to see
isolamento	isolation	viso	face
malattia	illness	vivo	alive
mal di mare	sea-sickness	voce (f)	voice
medico	doctor	volere	to want
medicamento	medicament, medicine	vomitare	to vomit
medicina	medicine		
medicinale	medicinal, medicine (R)		
meglio	better	**Accident**	
molto tempo, a lungo	long, a long while		
mordere	to bite	(moto) ciclista	(motor) cyclist
morire	to die	accusare	to accuse
morto	dead	aiutare	to help
occhiali	spectacles	all'improvviso	suddenly
operazione (f)	operation	ambulanza	ambulance
ora	hour, now	amico	friend
ospedale (m)	hospital	arrabbiarsi	to get angry
ottico	optician, optical	aspettare	to wait
otturazione (f)	filling	assicurato	insured
ovatta	cotton-wool	attenzione!	Look out!, Caution!
pastiglia	tablet	attraversare	to cross
paziente (m/f)	patient	autobus (m)	bus
piangere	to cry	autocarro	lorry
pillola	pill	avere il diritto	to have the right
pomata	ointment, cream	avere la precedenza	to have the right of way (R)
preoccuparsi	to worry, to be troubled	avere paura	to be afraid

Vocabulary

avvertire	to warn, to inform	incidente (m)	accident
bagnato	wet	indirizzo	address
barella	stretcher	informare	to inform
britannico	British	investire	to collide with, to run over
bruciare	to burn		
cabina telefonica	telephone box	investito	hit
cadere	to fall	là	there
camminare	to walk	macchina	car
carabiniere (m)	'carabiniere', 'policeman'	mamma mia!	dear me!, my goodness!
		marca	make (R)
carreggiata	carriage way	marciapiede (m)	pavement
carta d'identità	identity card	medico	doctor
caserma dei carabinieri	police station ('carabinieri')	mettere	to put
		mi scusi	excuse me; I'm sorry
certo	certainly	morto	dead
chiamare	to call	multa	fine
circolare	to drive round, to keep moving	nome (m)	name
		numero	number
codice (stradale) (m)	(highway) code (R)	ospedale (m)	hospital
collisione (f)	collision	pagare	to pay
colpa	fault	passante (m/f)	passer-by
commissariato	police station	passare	to pass
condurre	to drive, to lead	patente (f)	driving licence
conduttore (m)	driver	Pazienza!/Non importa!	Never mind!
consolato	consulate	pedone (m)	pedestrian
correre	to run, to speed	pericolo	danger
corriera	coach	permesso	permission
d'accordo	agreed	piangere	to cry
danno	damage	piano	gently, carefully
dichiarare	to declare	più tardi	later
dichiarazione (f)	statement (R)	polizia	police
domanda	question	polizza d'assicurazione	insurance policy
dopo	after	pompiere (m)	fireman
eppure	and yet (R)	posto di polizia	police station
falso	false	prego!	don't mention it!
fare attenzione	to be careful	presto!	quick!
fare	to do, to make	problema (m)	problem
ferito	wounded	prossimo	next
fermarsi	to stop	protestare	to protest
fortunatamente	luckily	purtroppo	unfortunately
fuoco, (al ...!)	fire, (fire!)	quasi	almost
girare	to turn	questura	police headquarters
grave	serious	qui, qua	here
gridare	to shout	rallentare	to slow down (R)
guardare	to watch	responsabile	responsible
guidatore (m)	driver	riempire/compilare	to fill in (R)
immediatamente	immediately	riparare	to repair (R)
improvvisamente	suddenly	rischio	risk

85

Vocabulary

rispettare	to respect
rovesciarsi	to overturn
sbrigarsi	to hurry up
scontro	collision, crash
scusare	to excuse
scusarsi	to apologize
semaforo	traffic lights
senso unico	one way
sicuro	sure, safe
slittare	to slide
sopralluogo	on the spot investigation (R)
sorpassare	to overtake
sorprendente	surprising (R)
sorpresa	surprise
spiacente	sorry
strada	road
subito	immediately
targa	number plate
telefonare	to telephone
testimone (m/f)	witness (R)
traversare	to cross
troppo presto	too soon
tutti	all
uccidere	to kill
urgente	urgent
urto	collision, impact
vedere	to see
veicolo	vehicle (R)
vero	true
vigili del fuoco	firemen
volere	to want

Abbreviations

C.R.I. Croce Rossa Italiana *Italian Red Cross*

I.N.P.S. Istituto Nazionale di Previdenza Sociale *National Institute of Social Insurance*

S.P.E. Soccorso Pubblico d'Emergenza *Public Emergency Assistance*

U.S.L. Unità Sanitaria Locale *Local Health Unit*

FREE TIME AND ENTERTAINMENT

andare a cavallo	to go on horseback, to ride
andare al mare	to go to the seaside
andare in bicicletta	to cycle
andare in campagna	to go to the countryside
andare in montagna	to go to the mountains
annoiarsi	to get bored
arte (f)	art
atletica	athletics
attore (m)	actor
ballare	to dance
biblioteca	library
biglietto	ticket
calcio (gioco del ...)	football
camminare	to walk
campeggio	camping site
campionato	championship
canna da pesca	fishing rod
cantante (m/f)	singer
cantare	to sing
canzone (f)	song
cartoni animati	cartoons
centro giovanile	youth club
chitarra	guitar
ciclismo	cycling
cinema (m)	cinema
circo	circus
collezionare	to collect
collezione (f)	collection
computer (m)	computer
concerto	concert
concorso	competition
dama	draughts
discoteca	discotheque
elefante (m)	elephant
elettronica	electronics
essere di moda	to be in fashion
fare la coda/la fila	to queue
fare un gol	to score a goal
fotografia	photography
gara	competition
giocare a pallone (bocce, carte)	to play football (bowls, cards)
giocare a dama	to play draughts
giocare a scacchi	to play chess
giornale (m)	newspaper

Vocabulary

gita	*excursion, trip*
gruppo	*group*
guida	*guide*
leggere	*to read*
leone (m)	*lion*
moda	*fashion*
museo	*museum*
musica classica	*classical music*
musica popolare	*folk music*
nuotare	*to swim*
nuoto	*swimming*
opera	*opera*
orchestra	*orchestra*
orso	*bear*
pallanuoto	*water-polo*
pallacanestro	*basket-ball*
pattini a rotelle	*roller-skates*
pattinare su ghiaccio	*to ice-skate*
pescare	*to fish*
pianoforte (m)	*piano*
piscina	*swimming pool*
pista	*rink, (ski) run, (dance) floor*
preferire	*to prefer*
programma (m)	*programme*
pugilato	*boxing*
quotidiano	*daily*
radio (f)	*radio*
ridere	*to laugh*
riunione (f)	*meeting*
rivista	*magazine*
scacchi	*chess*
sci	*skiing*
sciare	*to ski*
scimmia	*monkey*
sport acquatico	*water sport*
strumento musicale	*musical instrument*
svago	*amusement, recreation, hobby*
teatro	*theatre*
televisione (f)	*television*
tennis (m)	*tennis*
tigre (f)	*tiger*
tuffarsi	*to dive*
video	*video*
zoo	*zoo*

RELATIONS WITH OTHERS

General

amare	*to love, to like*
amico	*friend*
anche	*also*
andare	*to go*
apprezzare	*to appreciate*
ascoltare	*to listen to*
attività	*activity*
avere	*to have*
ballare	*to dance*
capire	*to understand*
capirsi	*to understand each other*
centro giovanile	*youth club*
circolo	*club*
club (m)	*club*
conoscere	*to know; to meet*
contento	*happy, glad*
di solito	*usually*
disco	*disc, record*
discutere	*to discuss*
divertirsi	*to enjoy oneself*
essere	*to be*
fare	*to make, to do*
frequentare	*to attend*
giocare	*to play*
giovane	*young*
gioventù (f)	*youth*
gruppo	*group*
interessarsi di	*to be interested in*
membro	*member*
musica	*music*
occuparsi di	*to occupy oneself with, to deal with*
parlare	*to talk, to speak*
partecipare	*to take part in*
passare	*to pass, to spend*
passatempo	*pastime, hobby*
pensare	*to think*
quando	*when*
quata (d'iscrizione)	*entrance fee (R)*
ringraziare	*to thank*
riunione (f)	*meeting*
sempre	*always*
socio	*member*
spesso	*often*

• •

tessera (d'iscrizione)	*membership card*
verità	*truth*

Making Acquaintances

accompagnare	*to accompany*
arrivederci	*goodbye*
assicurare	*to assure, ensure*
augurare	*to wish*
bene	*well*
benvenuto	*welcome*
buon anno	*happy new year*
buongiorno	*good morning*
buon viaggio	*have a good journey*
buona fortuna	*good luck*
buonanotte	*good night*
buonasera	*good evening*
collega (m/f)	*colleague*
come stai?, come sta? (formal)	*how are you?*
congratulazioni	*congratulations*
conoscente (m/f)	*acquaintance*
conoscenza	*acquaintance*
finalmente	*at last*
gente (f, sing.)	*people*
Inghilterra	*England*
inglese	*English*
insopportabile	*unbearable*
Italia	*Italy*
italiano	*Italian*
lettera	*letter*
persona	*person*
piacere!	*pleased to meet you!*
presentare	*to introduce*
ricambiare	*to return, to reciprocate*
vedersi	*to meet*

Arranging a meeting or an activity

a che ora?	*at what time?*
a destra	*on the right*
a domani	*see you tomorrow*
accettare	*to accept*
accompagnare	*to accompany*
allora	*then*
appuntamento	*appointment, date*
arrivare	*to arrive*
aspettare	*to wait*
avere il tempo di	*to have the time to*

bene	*well*
certamente	*of course, certainly*
cinema (m)	*cinema*
con piacere	*with pleasure*
costare	*to cost*
d'accordo	*agreed*
decidere	*to decide*
di buon'ora	*early*
di nuovo	*again*
dimenticare	*to forget*
dipende da	*it depends on*
domandare	*to ask*
domani	*tomorrow*
dove	*where*
dovere	*to have to, duty*
è necessario	*it is necessary*
esagerare	*to exaggerate, to go too far*
forse	*perhaps, may be*
gentile	*kind*
idea	*idea*
impossibile	*impossible*
in ritardo	*late*
incontrare	*to meet*
incontrarsi ancora	*to meet again*
insieme	*together*
intenzione (f)	*intention*
invitare	*to invite*
invito	*invitation*
libero	*free*
mattina	*morning*
mi dispiace di...	*I regret that..*
momento	*moment*
naturalmente	*of course, naturally*
non vale la pena	*it's not worth it*
non vedere l'ora di	*to look forward to*
offrire	*to offer*
parco	*park*
passeggiata	*walk*
peccato (che ...!)	*what a pity!*
perché	*why, because*
permesso	*permission*
piacere	*to like*
pomeriggio	*afternoon*
possibile	*possible*
preferire	*to prefer*
prima di	*before*
promettere	*to promise*

Vocabulary

proporre	to propose	inflazione (f)	inflation
prossimo	next	inquinamento	pollution
quasi	almost	libertà	freedom (R)
ragione (f)	reason	litigare	to argue
rifiutare	to refuse, to turn down		
sapere	to know, to be able to	manifestazione (f)	demonstration
scusarsi	to apologize	ministro	minister
sera/serata	evening	nazionalismo	nationalism (R)
settimana	week	ottimista	optimist
sorpresa	surprise	pace (f)	peace
suggerire	to suggest	parlamento	parliament
supporre	to suppose, to think	partito	party
televisione (f)	television	pessimista	pessimist
unico	only, unique	politica	politics, policy
uscire	to leave, to go out	povertà	poverty (R)
vedere	to see	presidente (m)	president
vedersi	to see, to meet	presidente del consiglio	prime minister
venire	to come	problema (m)	problem, issue
visto che	considering that	reddito	income
volentieri	willingly, gladly	ricchezza	wealth (R)
volere	to want, to wish	sciopero	strike
		sequestrare	to kidnap, to confiscate
		siccità	drought
		sindacato	trade union

Current affairs

ambiente (m)	environment	sinistra (di ...)	left-wing
attualità	current affairs	socialista	socialist
aumento	increase, rise	sviluppo	development
carestia	famine	tassa, imposta	tax
comunista	communist	terrorismo	terrorism
criminalità	crime	terzo mondo	third world
crisi	crisis	violenza	violence
debito	debt	votare	to vote
democratico	democratic		
destra (di ...)	right-wing		
dibattere	to debate		
disarmo	disarmament (R)		
discutere	to discuss		
disoccupato	unemployed		
ecologia	ecology		
elezione (f)	election		
emigrazione (f)	emigration		
energia	energy, power		
giustizia	justice		
governo	government		
guerra	war		
guerriglia	guerilla warfare		
inchiesta	investigation, inquiry (R)		

Major Political Parties & Trade Unions

D.C. Democrazia Cristiana *Christian Democrat Party*

M.S.I.-D.N. Movimento Sociale Italiano - Destra Nazionale *Italian Social Party - National Right*

P.C.I. Partito Comunista Italiano *Italian Communist Party*

P.L.I. Partito Liberale Italiano *Italian Liberal Party*

P.R. Partito Radicale *Radical Party*

P.R.I. Partito Repubblicano Italiano *Italian Republican Party*

P.S.DI. Partito Socialista Democratico
Italiano *Italian Socialist Democrat Party*
P.S.I Partito Socialista Italiano *Italian Socialist Party*

C.G.I.L Confederazione Generale Italiana
del Lavoro *General Federation of Italian Trade Unions*
C.I.S.L. Confederazione Italiana Sindacati
Lavoratori *Italian Federation of Trade Unions*
U.I.L. Unione Italiana del Lavoro *Italian Labour Union*

EDUCATION AND FUTURE CAREER

(see also Occupations)

abbastanza	*enough, quite, fairly*
abituarsi a	*to be accustomed to, to get used to*
abitudine (f)	*habit, custom*
accompagnare a scuola	*to take to school*
adesso	*now*
affari	*business*
agricoltore (m)	*farmer*
alunno	*pupil*
ambizione (f)	*ambition*
anche	*also, too*
anno	*year*
annoiarsi	*to be bored*
apprendere	*to learn*
arredatore (m)	*interior designer (R)*
arrivare	*to arrive*
artigiano	*craftsman*
ascoltare	*to listen to*
asilo (infantile)	*nursery*
assente	*absent*
attenzione; (ascoltare con ...)	*attention, to listen carefully*
attualmente	*at present, at the moment (R)*
aula	*classroom*
aver ragione/torto	*to be right/wrong*
avvenire (m)	*future*
ballo	*dance, ball*
banca	*bank*

banco	*desk*
bene	*well*
biblioteca	*library*
bisogna	*it is necessary that*
bocciare	*to fail*
borsa di studio	*grant, scholarship*
bravo (in)	*good (at)*
buono	*good*
calcio	*football*
campionato	*championship*
campione (m)	*champion*
capire	*to understand*
capitano	*captain*
carriera	*career*
carta, (un foglio di ...)	*paper, (a sheet of ...)*
cattedra	*teacher's desk*
certificato	*certificate*
chiedere	*to ask*
circolo	*club*
classe (f)	*class*
collegio	*boarding school*
colto	*well-educated*
come	*like, as, how*
cominciare	*to begin, to start*
commerciale	*commercial*
commercio	*commerce, trade*
compito	*homework*
condotta	*behaviour*
conoscere	*to know*
consigliare	*to advise, to recommend*
continuare	*to continue*
correggere	*to correct, to mark*
corretto	*correct*
corso; (... serale)	*course; (evening class)*
cortile (m)	*playground, courtyard (R)*
credere	*to believe*
cultura	*culture, education*
dare	*to give*
debole (in)	*weak (in)*
decoratore (m)	*decorator*
dentista (m/f)	*dentist*
detestare	*to detest, to hate*
difficile	*difficult*
difficoltà	*difficulty*
dipende da ...	*depends on*
diploma (...di maturità) (m)	*diploma, (school leaving certificate)*

Vocabulary

direttore (m)	*headmaster*	**ingegnere (m)**	*engineer*
direttrice (f)	*headmistress*	**insegnante (m/f)**	*teacher*
disoccupato	*unemployed*	insegnare	*to teach*
disoccupazione	*unemployment*	intelligente	*intelligent*
diventare/divenire	*to become*	**intendere**	*to understand*
divertente	*amusing, funny*	interessante	*interesting*
divertirsi	*to enjoy oneself*	**interessare**	*to interest*
dopo	*after*	**interessarsi di**	*to be interested in*
dovere	*duty, to have to*	intervallo	*break*
dubbio (senza ...)	*doubt (no ...)*	**iscrizione (f)**	*enrolment*
durare	*to last*	**istruito**	*educated, learned*
durata	*duration, length*	istruzione (f)	*education*
educazione (f)	*upbringing*	laboratorio	*laboratory, work shop*
elementare; (scuola ...)	*elementary; (primary school)*	lasciare	*to leave*
		laurea	*degree*
errore; (... d'ortografia) (m)	*mistake, error; (spelling mistake)*	**laurearsi**	*to graduate*
		lavagna	*blackboard*
esame (m)	*exam*	lavorare	*to work*
esempio	*example*	lavoro; (... manuale)	*work, job; (manual work)*
estero (all' ...)	*abroad*	leggere	*to read*
età	*age*	lettura	*reading*
fabbrica	*factory*	lezione (f)	*lesson*
facile	*easy*	libro	*book*
fare	*to make, to do*	**liceo, (... classico, scientifico)**	*'liceo', (classical, scientific 'lycée')*
finire	*to finish*		
forse	*perhaps*	lingua	*language*
frase (f)	*sentence, phrase*	maestro	*(primary) teacher*
frequentare	*to attend*	matita	*pencil*
futuro	*future*	media	*average*
gesso	*chalk*	mensa	*canteen*
ginnasio	*first two years of 'classical lycée'*	molto	*much*
		necessario	*necessary*
giocare	*to play*	negozio	*shop*
gioco	*game*	noioso	*boring*
giornata	*day*	nuotare	*to swim*
gita	*trip, outing*	nuoto	*swimming*
gomma	*rubber*	**obbligatorio**	*compulsory*
gruppo	*group*	ogni	*every*
guaio	*trouble, difficulty*	opinione (f)	*opinion*
guardare	*to look*	ora	*hour, time*
imparare	*to learn*	orario	*timetable*
impiegato	*employee*	ottimo	*very good, excellent*
impiego	*employment, job*	paga	*pay, wage*
impossibile	*impossible*	pagina	*page*
inchiostro	*ink*	**palestra**	*gymnasium*
indicare	*to indicate, to show*	palla	*ball*
indovinare	*to guess*	pallone (m)	*foot-ball*
infine	*at last, finally*	partita	*match, game*

passatempo	pastime, hobby	**scelta**	choice
perché	why, because	scientifico	scientific
permesso	permission	**sciocco**	silly
permettere	to permit, to allow	scolaro	pupil, school boy
personale (m)	staff, personnel	scoperta	discovery
piacere	pleasure; to like	**scopo**	purpose, aim
piscina	swimming pool	scoprire	to discover, to find out
pittura	painting, paint	**scorretto**	incorrect
più	more	scrivere	to write
poco	little, not much	scuola privata	private school
poesia	poetry, poem	scuola pubblica/statale	State school
poeta (m)	poet	scuola media	first three years of
poi	then, later		secondary school
possibilità	possibility	**segretario**	secretary
posto; (...di lavoro)	place, space; (job)	sera	evening
preferire	to prefer	severo	strict
presente	present	**sforzarsi di**	to make an effort
preside (m/f)	headmaster/mistress	società	society, club
problema (m)	problem, issue	**sodo**	hard
professione (f)	profession, occupation	sperare	to hope
professore (m)	teacher, professor	spiegare	to explain
professoressa	teacher, professor	sport (m)	sport
progresso	progress	**stare**	to stay
promuovere	to pass	straniero	foreigner, foreign
provare	to try	strumento	instrument
punire	to punish	studente (m), studentessa	student
punizione (f)	punishment	studiare	to study
quaderno	exercise book	studio	study
quando	when	studioso	studious
quanto	how much	suonare	to ring, to play
raccontare	to tell	tardi (più ...)	later
racconto	story	teatro	theatre, drama
restare	to stay	tema (m)	essay, composition
ricreazione (f)	recreation, break (R)	tennis (m)	tennis
righello	ruler	**tradurre**	to translate
ripetere	to repeat	traduzione (f)	translation
rispondere	to reply	trovare	to find
risultato	result, answer	tutto	all
ritardo	late	**ubbidire**	to obey
ritorno	return	uniforme	uniform
romanzo	novel	università	university
salario	salary, wage (R)	vacanza	holiday
sapere	to know	vero	true
sbaglio	mistake	**vincere**	to win
scadente	unsatisfactory, poor quality (R)	vita	life
		vocabolario	vocabulary
scambio	exchange	**voglia; (aver ... di)**	wish; (to feel like)
scegliere	to choose	volere	to want, to wish

Vocabulary

voto, (aver voti belli/brutti) *mark (to have good/bad marks)*

Subjects

biologia	*biology*
ceramica	*pottery*
chimica	*chemistry*
dattilografia	*typing*
economia	*economics*
educazione artistica	*art*
educazione civica	*civics*
educazione fisica	*physical education*
educazione musicale	*music*
educazione tecnica	*technical education*
elettronica	*electronics*
fisica	*physics*
francese (m)	*French*
geografia	*geography*
greco	*Greek*
inglese (m)	*English*
italiano	*Italian*
latino	*Latin*
letteratura	*literature*
lingue moderne	*modern languages*
matematica	*maths*
morale (f)	*ethics*
musica	*music*
ragioneria	*accounting*
religione (f)	*religious education*
scienze (f, pl.)	*science*
scienze naturali	*natural sciences*
scienze umane	*human sciences*
sociologia	*sociology*
spagnolo	*Spanish*
stenografia	*shorthand*
storia dell'arte	*history of art*
storia	*history*
teatro	*drama*
tedesco	*German*

VERB TABLE

INDICATIVE (INDICATIVO)

	ESSERE	AVERE	ABITARE	RIPETERE	PARTIRE
PRESENT					
(io)	sono	ho	abito	ripeto	parto
(tu)	sei	hai	abiti	ripeti	parti
(lui, lei, Lei)	è	ha	abita	ripete	parte
(noi)	siamo	abbiamo	abitiamo	ripetiamo	partiamo
(voi)	siete	avete	abitate	ripetete	partite
(loro)	sono	hanno	abitano	ripetono	partono
PERFECT					
	sono stato/a	ho avuto	ho abitato	ho ripetuto	sono partito/a
	sei stato/a	hai avuto	hai abitato	hai ripetuto	sei partito/a
	è stato/a	ha avuto	ha abitato	ha ripetuto	è partito/a
	siamo stati/e	abbiamo avuto	abbiamo abitato	abbiamo ripetuto	siamo partiti/e
	siete stati/e	avete avuto	avete abitato	avete ripetuto	siete partiti/e
	sono stati/e	hanno avuto	hanno abitato	hanno ripetuto	sono partiti/e
IMPERFECT					
	ero	avevo	abitavo	ripetevo	partivo
	eri	avevi	abitavi	ripetevi	partivi
	era	aveva	abitava	ripeteva	partiva
	eravamo	avevamo	abitavamo	ripetevamo	partivamo
	eravate	avevate	abitavate	ripetevate	partivate
	erano	avevano	abitavano	ripetevano	partivano
PLUPERFECT					
	ero stato/a	avevo avuto	avevo abitato	avevo ripetuto	ero partito/a
	eri stato/a	avevi avuto	avevi abitato	avevi ripetuto	eri partito/a
	era stato/a	aveva avuto	aveva abitato	aveva ripetuto	era partito/a
	eravamo stati/e	avevamo avuto	avevamo abitato	avevamo ripetuto	eravamo partiti/e
	eravate stati/e	avevate avuto	avevate abitato	avevate ripetuto	eravate partiti/e
	erano stati/e	avevano avuto	avevano abitato	avevano ripetuto	erano partiti/e

	ESSERE	AVERE	ABITARE	RIPETERE	PARTIRE
PAST HISTORIC					
	fui	ebbi	abitai	ripetei	partii
	fosti	avesti	abitasti	ripetesti	partisti
	fu	ebbe	abitò	ripeté	partì
	fummo	avemmo	abitammo	ripetemmo	partimmo
	foste	aveste	abitaste	ripeteste	partiste
	furono	ebbero	abitarono	ripeterono	partirono
PAST ANTERIOR					
	fui stato/a	ebbi avuto	ebbi abitato	ebbi ripetuto	fui partito/a
	fosti stato/a	avesti avuto	avesti abitato	avesti ripetuto	fosti partito/a
	fu stato/a	ebbe avuto	ebbe abitato	ebbe ripetuto	fu partito/a
	fummo stati/e	avemmo avuto	avemmo abitato	avemmo ripetuto	fummo partiti/e
	foste stati/e	aveste avuto	aveste abitato	aveste ripetuto	foste partiti/e
	furono stati/e	ebbero avuto	ebbero abitato	ebbero ripetuto	furono partiti/e
FUTURE					
	sarò	avrò	abiterò	ripeterò	partirò
	sarai	avrai	abiterai	ripeterai	partirai
	sarà	avrà	abiterà	ripeterà	partirà
	saremo	avremo	abiteremo	ripeteremo	partiremo
	serete	avrete	abiterete	ripeterete	partirete
	saranno	avranno	abiteranno	ripeteranno	partiranno
FUTURE PERFECT					
	sarò stato/a	avrò avuto	avrò abitato	avrò ripetuto	sarò partito/a
	sarai stato/a	avrai avuto	avrai abitato	avrai ripetuto	sarai partito/a
	sarà stato/a	avrà avuto	avrà abitato	avrà ripetuto	sarà partito/a
	saremo stati/e	avremo avuto	avremo abitato	avremo ripetuto	saremo partiti/e
	sarete stati/e	avrete avuto	avrete abitato	avrete ripetuto	sarete partiti/e
	saranno stati/e	avranno avuto	avranno abitato	avranno ripetuto	saranno partiti/e

SUBJUNCTIVE (CONGIUNTIVO)

	ESSERE	AVERE	ABITARE	RIPETERE	PARTIRE
PRESENTE	sia	abbia	abiti	ripeta	parta
	sia	abbia	abiti	ripeta	parta
	sia	abbia	abiti	ripeta	parta
	siamo	abbiamo	abitiamo	ripetiamo	partiamo
	siate	abbiate	abitiate	ripetiate	partiate
	siano	abbiano	abitino	ripetano	partano
PAST	sia stato/a	abbia avuto	abbia abitato	abbia ripetuto	sia partito/a
	sia stato/a	abbia avuto	abbia abitato	abbia ripetuto	sia partito/a
	sia stato/a	abbia avuto	abbia abitato	abbia ripetuto	sia partito/a
	siamo stati/e	abbiamo avuto	abbiamo abitato	abbiamo ripetuto	siamo partiti/e
	siate stati/e	abbiate avuto	abbiate abitato	abbiate ripetuto	siate partiti/e
	siano stati/e	abbiano avuto	abbiano abitato	abbiano ripetuto	siano partiti/e
IMPERFECT	fossi	avessi	abitassi	ripetessi	partissi
	fossi	avessi	abitassi	ripetessi	partissi
	fosse	avesse	abitasse	ripetesse	partisse
	fossimo	avessimo	abitassimo	ripetessimo	partissimo
	foste	aveste	abitaste	ripeteste	partiste
	fossero	avessero	abitassero	ripetessero	partissero
PLUPERFECT	fossi stato/a	avessi avuto	avessi abitato	avessi ripetuto	fossi partito/a
	fossi stato/a	avessi avuto	avessi abitato	avessi ripetuto	fossi partito/a
	fosse stato/a	avesse avuto	avesse abitato	avesse ripetuto	fosse partito/a
	fossimo stati/e	avessimo avuto	avessimo abitato	avessimo ripetuto	fossimo partiti/e
	foste stati/e	aveste avuto	aveste abitato	aveste ripetuto	foste partiti/e
	fossero stati/e	avessero avuto	avessero abitato	avessero ripetuto	fossero partiti/e

CONDITIONAL (CONDIZIONALE)

PRESENT				
sarei	avrei	abiterei	ripeterei	partirei
saresti	avresti	abiteresti	ripeteresti	partiresti
sarebbe	avrebbe	abiterebbe	ripeterebbe	partirebbe
saremmo	avremmo	abiteremmo	ripeteremmo	partiremmo
sareste	avreste	abitereste	ripetereste	partireste
sarebbero	avrebbero	abiterebbero	ripeterebbero	partirebbero

PAST				
sarei stato/a	avrei avuto	avrei abitato	avrei ripetuto	sarei partito/a
saresti stato/a	avresti avuto	avresti abitato	avresti ripetuto	saresti partito/a
sarebbe stato/a	avrebbe avuto	avrebbe abitato	avrebbe ripetuto	sarebbe partito/a
saremmo stati/e	avremmo avuto	avremmo abitato	avremmo ripetuto	saremmo partiti/e
sareste stati/e	avreste avuto	avreste abitato	avreste ripetuto	sareste partiti/e
sarebbero stati/e	avrebbero avuto	avrebbero abitato	avrebbero ripetuto	sarebbero partiti/e

IMPERATIVE (IMPERATIVO)

sii (tu)	abbi	abita	ripeti	parti
sia (Lei)	abbia	abiti	ripeta	parta
siamo (noi)	abbiamo	abitiamo	ripetiamo	partiamo
siate (voi)	abbiate	abitate	ripetete	partite
siano (Loro)	abbiano	abitino	ripetano	partano

GERUND (GERUNDIO)

PRESENT	essendo	avendo	abitando	ripetendo	partendo
PAST	essendo stato/a/i/e	avendo avuto	avendo abitato	avendo ripetuto	essendo partito/a/i/e

PARTICIPLE (PARTICIPIO)

PRESENT	(essente)	avente	abitante	ripetente	partente
PAST	stato/a/i/e	avuto	abitato	ripetuto	partito

INFINITIVE (INFINITO)

PRESENT	essere	avere	abitare	ripetere	partire
PERFECT	essere stato/a/i/e	avere avuto	avere abitato	avere ripetuto	essere partito/a/i/e

Index

Index

Index